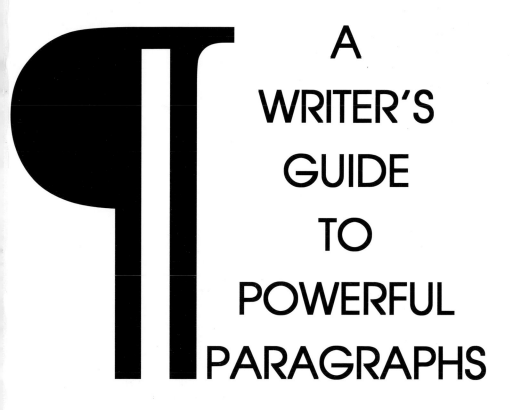

A WRITER'S GUIDE TO POWERFUL PARAGRAPHS

Victor C. Pellegrino

Maui arThoughts Company
P.O. Box 967, Wailuku, HI, USA 96793-0967
Phone or Fax: 808-244-0156
Phone or Fax Orders Toll Free: 800-403-3472
E-mail: books@maui.net
Website: www.booksmaui.com

Publisher's Cataloging-in-Publication Data
(Provided by Quality Books, Inc.)

Pellegrino, Victor C.
    A writer's guide to powerful paragraphs / Victor C.
    Pellegrino. -- 1st ed.
        p. cm.
        Includes index.
        LCCN 2002109852
        ISBN 0-945045-05-0

    1. English language--Paragraphs. I. Title

PE1439.P45 2003   808'.042
                             QBI02-200563

Pellegrino, Victor C.
A Writer's Guide to Powerful Paragraphs
International Standard Book Number: 0-945045-05-0
Library of Congress Control Number: 2002109852
Copyright © 2003 by Maui arThoughts Company
2nd Printing, 2009
All rights reserved
Printed in Korea

Icons: Christopher Magee, Graphic Artist
Pen point cover graphic: Hemera Technologies, Inc.
Printing: AMICA International, Kent, WA

Published by
Maui arThoughts Company
P.O. Box 967, Wailuku, HI, USA 96793-0967
Phone or Fax: 808-244-0156
Phone or Fax Orders: 800-403-3472
E-mail: books@maui.net
Website: www.booksmaui.com

DEDICATION

To my wife

Wallette Pualani Lyn-fah

To my children

Shelley Jeanne Laʻelaʻeokalā Lyn-oi
Angela Terese Mahinamālamalama Mei-lyn
Hōkūao Christopher Joseph Bailey Wu-wei

To my parents

Albert and Adeline Pellegrino

ACKNOWLEDGMENTS

A Writer's Guide to Powerful Paragraphs has been in the process of creation for several years. During that time, many special people have provided me with support and guidance.

I am most specially grateful to David Merchant and Shelley Pellegrino, who painstakingly edited and proofread the chapters. Their diligent efforts, constructive changes, and love for writing turned the manuscript into a book of which I am proud.

I am also grateful to Angela Pellegrino for the creative assistance and direction she provided for the cover design, graphics, and layout.

My wife, Wallette, deserves so much gratitude for having supported me throughout the writing of this book—and seven others. She provides a kind and careful eye and sincere comments, which I always welcome.

Many people from different professions and backgrounds have reviewed this book. I am especially grateful—and humbled—to have received such glowing testimonials from Claire Kamasaki, Professor of English, Middlesex Community College; Regina Lehnhoff, English Department Chair, Marian High School; Andrew Pudewa, Director, Institute for Excellence in Writing; Dr. Joyce Trafton, Collegiate Professor, Education, University of Maryland; and Debbie Hasegawa Winkler, Acting Director, The Learning Center, Maui Community College.

I want to extend special thanks to Christopher Magee, Visiting Assistant Professor in Animation at the

University of the Arts, Philadelphia, for creating the chapter icons. This is my second book for which Chris has designed icons, and I continue to appreciate his creativity and imagination.

I also wish to acknowledge the dedication and professionalism of Aziz Junejo and Rizwan Awan of AMICA International, Kent, Washington. Besides being excellent printers and business people, they understand an author's perspective.

Finally, I wish to thank the hundreds of students of writing I have had the pleasure of teaching. Because of them, my writing is what it is.

CONTENTS

PREFACE

Writing is something almost everyone must do, and do well. Writing well requires more than putting words on paper. Writing is best when it is concise, meaningful, and easily understood. This book is written with these objectives in mind. It is designed for writers of all ages and backgrounds who want to improve their writing.

If you are in school, this book will help you master basic paragraph writing skills that you can apply to longer pieces of writing. If you are entering the workforce, this book will be a useful reference tool to reinforce what you learned in school. If you have not written in a while, this book will help refresh your writing skills. If you have been recently promoted, changed jobs, or simply want to improve your writing, this book can add polish to your existing skills.

Most of today's communication is brief. Letters, notes, memos, faxes, and e-mails are generally short and to the point—sometimes only a paragraph or two. Writing briefly, however, does not mean you can ignore the hallmarks of good writing. Whether you are writing a long or short piece, your main focus should be clarity, brevity, and understandability. Writers should not rush. A common mistake writers make when using today's shorter styles is to rush through the writing process without organizing, proofreading, or editing.

To help you improve your writing, *A Writer's Guide to Powerful Paragraphs* focuses on how to organize the shortest piece of writing that can stand alone—the paragraph. The heart of this book lies in the thirty chapters that provide thirty different ways to write paragraphs. Each chapter contains a short, simple, and direct explanation of one type of paragraph, followed by an example, an analysis of the example, and practical suggestions for writing that type of paragraph.

A Writer's Guide to Powerful Paragraphs is a "hands-on" book. Rather than force you to wade through fine print and a lot of complicated textbook-like instruction, this book uses short discussions followed by practical examples. After you read and study the paragraph type outlined in each chapter, practice writing that type of paragraph. Then let someone else critique your work; there is no better method to improve your writing than to have it reviewed by a friendly, but critical, eye. Hopefully, this process will make learning about paragraph writing painless and enjoyable.

Finally, although this book focuses on structuring your paragraph in one of thirty ways, do not think that you have to limit yourself to just one paragraph type. Good writers will be able to combine two or more. So once you have a good handle on each of the paragraph types, experiment by using more than one within a paragraph or in multiple paragraphs.

As writers, we combine words to make sentences, we combine sentences to make paragraphs, and we use multiple paragraphs to create essays, chapters, and books. Once you have mastered the paragraph, you are on your way. Experiment. Create. Enjoy.

Good writing,
Victor C. Pellegrino
Waikapū, Maui, Hawai'i
2009

HOW TO USE
THIS BOOK

    A Writer's Guide to Powerful Paragraphs is designed to be simple and easy to use. If you have not done so already, I recommend that you read the *Preface* and scan the *Contents*. Reading these sections will provide a sense of the goals of this book and a road map of how it will try to achieve those goals. I recommend reviewing these sections not because I wish to insult my audience, but because so many readers tend to neglect the importance of previewing a book in their haste to get into the content. In doing so, they fail to understand the "big picture" of a book.

    Next, read and study the seven sections listed under *The Paragraph*. Some of this material may be familiar to you, depending on your age or writing experience, and some of it may be new. In either case, these seven sections will set the foundation for what is to follow, and make learning the thirty different methods less complicated and more enjoyable.

    After you have reviewed the foundation chapters, it is time to move to the heart of the book—the thirty paragraph types. These thirty structures will help you write a variety of paragraphs. Each chapter is laid out similarly and contains the following sections: (1) a short explanation of the paragraph type; (2) a sample paragraph; (3) an analysis of the sample paragraph; and (4) practical suggestions for writing that type of paragraph.

I have tried to avoid formal terminology—what I call "scholarly gobbledygook"—as well as complex content. After all, the purpose of this book is not to camouflage or obscure information, but to show simply and directly how you can master basic paragraph writing skills.

While I certainly hope you benefit by studying this book, the best advice I can give anyone who wants to improve his or her writing skills is this: Practice. Practice. Practice. Use the models in this book as a springboard to create your own paragraphs. After you are able to write individual paragraphs using the basic structures, practice combining different paragraph structures within a larger piece of writing.

An equally important part of writing practice is sharing. Writing is meant to be read, so share your paragraphs with others. Listen to feedback and do not be afraid to restructure your ideas. Once you learn the value of writing and revising, you will become a much better writer.

Finally, as you begin to combine your paragraphs into larger pieces of writing, you will want to make the paragraphs flow together. Two excellent books that will be helpful to this process are *A Writer's Guide to Transitional Words and Expressions* and *A Writer's Guide to Using Eight Methods of Transition*.

A WRITER'S GUIDE
TO
POWERFUL
PARAGRAPHS

THE PARAGRAPH

History
Definition, Signal and Function
Length and Development
Topic Sentence
Unity
Coherence
Planning and Organizing

HISTORY

The paragraph as we know it is a surprisingly new creation. Although writers have long recognized the need to organize their work into manageable pieces, there was no standard method for doing so until the middle of the 1800s.

The idea of using individual units of thought as the organizing method for writing can be attributed to Scottish educator Alexander Bain (1818-1903). As a teacher at Aberdeen University, Bain studied and wrote about a wide variety of subjects, including English grammar, rhetoric, philosophy, logic, psychology, ethics, and education. He was a true believer in the democratic ideal of educating the masses.

Bain's wide studies, particularly his focus on logic and writing, led him to introduce the modern paragraph in 1866. He believed that the paragraph, which he defined as a single unit of thought, provided writers with a way both to break down large ideas into a series of smaller ideas and to make sure that each smaller idea got the attention it deserved. Bain stressed the importance of using a topic sentence in each paragraph to properly develop and define the idea covered in the paragraph. Finally, as a signal to the reader that "a new idea begins here," Bain used an indentation at the beginning of each paragraph. All of these features remain important today.

Alexander Bain, from the viewpoint of writers and readers alike, made an invaluable contribution to composition. The paragraph has made explaining ideas an easier process for the writer as well as understanding them an easier process for the reader.

DEFINITION,
SIGNAL AND FUNCTION

The paragraph is a unit of thought, expressing a single idea, communicated through related sentences. One way to think about a paragraph is to compare it with an orange. An orange has several distinct sections connected to each other to form a whole fruit. All of the sections share a common center. A paragraph has distinct parts too, called sentences. Some sentences follow each other naturally, while others must be connected by transitional words or expressions. Like the parts of an orange, all of these sentences relate to a common center. The common center of a paragraph contains the main idea of the paragraph and is called the topic sentence.

The paragraph is a clever invention that allows writers to place thoughts related to a single idea into a single block of writing. By keeping thoughts related to one idea together, paragraphs allow readers to concentrate on one idea at a time and understand that idea before moving on to the next. For some writers, settling on a single idea and keeping together thoughts related to that idea come naturally; for others, the process of determining where one idea ends and the next one begins takes practice.

Writers signal the beginning of a new idea by indenting the first line of each new paragraph. The indent is usually one inch when writing by hand, five spaces when using a typewriter, and one-half inch when using a computer. (In some business letters, writers do not indent, but instead signal their readers by double spacing between paragraphs.) What a perfect idea indenting is, because a reader can always know by a visual signal that the writer is saying, "Note, reader, I am beginning a new idea here."

To understand the function of the paragraph, ask yourself these questions: "What would writing be like if there were no paragraphs?" or "How would readers respond if they could not distinguish the end of one idea and the beginning of another?" Before you consider the answers to these questions, recall that the purpose of any writing is to convey ideas. Remember, too, that writers and readers are physically apart, and the only connection they have to each other is the printed page. Without paragraphs, readers would be forced to sift through sentences to find where ideas begin and end, and then try to group related thoughts and ideas together in their own minds. Most readers probably would become frustrated and give up trying. The end result would be failed communication. Good paragraphs eliminate this problem and ease the frustrations of both writing and reading.

Finally, remember that writing paragraphs, whether it comes naturally or takes a great amount of effort, is a process. Expect to revise your paragraphs. Revisions can include adding or eliminating sentences, shifting sentences within a paragraph, moving one or more sentences to other paragraphs, or connecting sentences with transitional words or expressions. Your goal as a writer is to communicate. Making the effort to write good, clear paragraphs will help you achieve your goal.

LENGTH
AND
DEVELOPMENT

Writers frequently ask, "How long should a paragraph be?" There is no simple answer to this question because there is no set formula to follow regarding paragraph length.

Paragraph length should not be dictated by a certain number of words or sentences. It is controlled by a main idea and as few or as many words as necessary for support and development. Once you have established your main idea and fully developed it, then your paragraph is complete. Thus, avoid formulas such as "a paragraph should be 150 words," or "a good length for a paragraph is seven sentences."

The first step in developing your paragraph is to decide on the idea to be communicated by the paragraph. Remember, each paragraph should contain only one main idea, so you must decide whether your topic is one idea that can be communicated in one paragraph, or two ideas that require two paragraphs. For example, "I have a comfortable apartment," is a single idea that would probably make a good paragraph. In contrast, "I have a comfortable apartment and a great car" are really two ideas that probably require two paragraphs—one about the apartment and one about the car.

Once you have identified your main idea, then you can begin writing your paragraph. Think of a paragraph as a series of interrelated sentences. The most important sentence is called the topic sentence and contains the main idea. You generally should begin by writing the topic sentence, even if it will not be the first sentence in your paragraph. Next, develop your topic sentence with supporting sentences that provide reasons, details, or examples. Once you have developed the topic sentence fully through supporting sentences, then your paragraph can stand on its own and you are ready to move on.

There are no set formulas to control paragraph length and development, but there are a few pointers to keep in mind. For instance, one good way to determine paragraph length is to rely on the major–minor principle: a major subject requires developing a relatively long paragraph; a minor subject requires developing a relatively short paragraph.

Even if you are addressing a minor idea in a relatively short paragraph, however, make sure you fully develop your idea. One of the most common errors writers make is that they fail to develop an idea to its full extent. The resulting paragraph reads like a bare, unsupported statement, and the reader is left with unanswered questions and an "unfinished" feeling. There are a number of steps you can take before writing that will help you avoid this problem. First, make sure you have sufficient information. Second, make sure you understand your subject fully. If necessary, you may have to do more research. Third, make sure you analyze your audience. Do not assume your audience knows more than it actually does.

Once you begin writing and set forth your main idea in a topic sentence, make sure that you provide enough information and examples in your remaining sentences to explain and support the topic sentence. Ask yourself if there is anything more that a reader must know to understand your main idea. Are there any assumptions you have made that should be explained? Is there some background information that you should supply? Would an example help? Ultimately, the test is whether the reader can fully understand your main idea. If your paragraph is developed, you will succeed in this test. If your paragraph is undeveloped and the reader is left with questions, you will not succeed very well at being either a convincing or effective communicator.

In summary, the keys to a good paragraph—whether long or short—are deciding on an idea for that paragraph and fully developing it. If you remember to state your single, main idea clearly and support it with sufficient descriptions, explanations, or arguments, your paragraph will be effective regardless of its length.

TOPIC SENTENCE

Once a writer has selected a topic, narrowed it down to material appropriate for one paragraph, and decided who the audience will be, it is time to begin writing. The first step in actually writing a paragraph is to state the main idea clearly and simply. The writer states this main idea in a topic sentence. The topic sentence is usually the first sentence, and it is always the core of the paragraph which other sentences support.

As the core of the paragraph, the topic sentence serves five functions. First, it tells the reader what the paragraph will be about. Second, it defines the size of the paragraph by presenting an idea broad enough to require description, argumentation, or explanation, but narrow enough to be dealt with in single paragraph. Third, it shapes the structure of the paragraph, defining whether the paragraph will present ideas from simple to complex, from least to most important, in chronological order, or in some other structure. Fourth, it shapes the tone a piece of writing will take (e.g., humorous, serious, sarcastic). Fifth, it helps the writer focus on individual pieces of information (paragraphs), either by themselves or as part of a larger work (composition or essay).

Writing simple and clear topic sentences is extremely important to good writing. It is also a skill that takes practice. Keep the following in mind when you write your topic sentences:

- Limit your topic sentence to one idea.

- Avoid confusing or ambiguous language in your topic sentence.

- Make the topic sentence a declarative sentence such as, "My dog Koa is courageous."

- If you begin your paragraph with a question, the question should lead to your declarative topic sentence.

- Avoid using an exclamatory sentence such as, "Angela's car is awesome!" as a topic sentence.

- Avoid the "I think" topic sentence, such as "I think America needs better laws regarding gun control." The reader knows that you are the writer and that the views or ideas you present are your own, so drop the "I think" and get on with the statement.

- Avoid topic sentences that begin with "I am going to write about…" or "I am going to tell you about…."

- Avoid using common adjectives in the topic sentence such as exciting, interesting, good, bad, or fun. These overused words create subjects that are too broad for development in one paragraph.

- Avoid writing topic sentences that use words such as everyone, anyone, all, nobody, no one, every, always, and never. Topic sentences containing these all-inclusive words are difficult to explain or prove, particularly in a single paragraph.

TOPIC SENTENCE

- Generally, the topic sentence comes first. While it is permissible to place the topic sentence in the middle or at the end of a paragraph, you should do so only in very specific instances and with a clear plan.

- A good topic sentence limits the subject and controls the length of a paragraph. If you find yourself writing a paragraph that never seems to end, your subject is probably too large. Go back and revise the topic sentence to narrow the subject of the paragraph. If you have trouble finding detail and support for your topic sentence, your subject is probably too narrow. Go back and revise your topic sentence to broaden the subject of the paragraph.

- Instead of being stated in a single sentence, your topic can be implied through a series of sentences. By presenting ideas and details in this way, you allow the reader to deduce the ideas you are writing about. This can be very tricky, as the reader may not grasp your implied topic and wonder why you have written a list of seemingly unconnected sentences. Therefore, before you use a more advanced technique such as this, make sure that you have mastered writing basic topic sentences.

UNITY

Unity refers to togetherness or oneness. Paragraph unity means the paragraph stands together as a single, well-developed idea. Unity is one of the most important characteristics of good writing because it provides a sense of understanding for the reader. With unity, the sentences in a paragraph flow naturally from one thought to the next; without unity, a paragraph seems to be just a series of disconnected, disjointed, and unrelated thoughts.

A writer achieves paragraph unity when all of the sentences in a paragraph relate to the main idea stated in the topic sentence. The reader is led from the topic sentence through related supporting sentences, all the while understanding how each supporting sentence relates to the topic sentence. As a result, the reader is left with a sense of understanding both the big picture of the topic sentence and the little pictures of the supporting sentences.

In contrast, a paragraph without unity will be jarring and confusing. The reader will not know why each sentence is in the paragraph and how each relates to the main idea.

One way to think about unity is to use the example of the orange introduced earlier. Even after you peel and divide an orange into separate sections, you can see that all of the sections are still part of the original orange. This is unity. Lack of unity occurs when you put an apple slice and a pear slice in with the orange sections. The reader thinks there should be some connection but is not quite sure what it is (Fruit? Slices? Food? Things that grow on trees?). Unless you can show clear relationships among the three subjects, you will confuse your reader.

You can achieve paragraph unity by following several important rules:

- Keep ideas together. Write about only one subject in each paragraph.

- Think of unity as "sticking to" your subject. Make every sentence "stick to" the topic sentence. Plan every paragraph by outlining the details and checking to see that they relate to the topic sentence. Revise or delete any sentence that fails this "stick to" test.

- Keep your paragraphs fairly short, particularly if you are having trouble with unity. The longer the paragraph, the more likely you will stray from your topic sentence by writing about unnecessary or unrelated things.

- If your paragraph wanders because it is too long, go back and revise the topic sentence. Try dividing it into two or more parts, and turn those parts into new topic sentences for shorter and more focused paragraphs.

COHERENCE

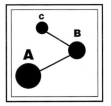

Coherence means making clear connections between sentences. Clear connections allow readers to perceive relationships among the sentences in a paragraph.

Coherence is closely related to unity. Remember that unity means that the thoughts in each sentence in a paragraph relate to a single idea. Coherence refers to connecting those sentences so the reader can understand exactly how they relate to the topic sentence and to each other. For example, you could use "first, next, after that," to connect ideas that focus on chronology, or "initially, next, even more important, most important" to connect ideas that focus on writing in climactic order. In short, coherence helps the reader follow the writer's chain of reasoning.

Because unity and coherence are so closely related, a good writer begins by making sure a paragraph has unity. Without unity, it will be impossible to have coherence; there is no writer's technique that coherently joins thoughts that do not belong together. Once the paragraph has unity, then the writer achieves coherence by using transitional connectors to guide the reader from point to point. If successful, a reader will see how each sentence is a separate thought that logically supports and builds upon the main idea.

To write with coherence, a writer must master specific transitional methods to join sentences together. The primary methods of transition are organized into eight main groups. Studying and practicing these eight methods will help you achieve the main goal of all good writing—clear and understandable communication.

1 – Use Transitional Words and Expressions

Transitional words and expressions are signal words that tell the reader you are moving from one point to the next. When you connect sentences and paragraphs in this way, you help readers see the relationships between points.

While transitional words and expressions are extremely helpful, you should keep in mind two things when using them. First, choose transitions wisely; selecting transitional words and expressions should not be the result of guesswork. Determine the relationship between the two sentences you are trying to connect and then decide which transitional word or phrase to use. Second, use transitions sparingly; if you use too many transitional words, they lose their effectiveness and your writing becomes cluttered and dull.

Listed below are a few of the many transitional words and expressions available to you. For a complete listing of more than one thousand transitional words and expressions, use *A Writer's Guide to Transitional Words and Expressions*.

- To indicate time order (e.g., earlier, later, now, in the past, not long ago).

- To indicate how or when something occurs in time (e.g., frequently, as soon as, rarely, as long as).

- To indicate sequence (e.g., to begin with, following that, next, last).

- To repeat (e.g., to put it differently, in other words, once again).

- To provide an example (e.g., for example, to illustrate, in this instance).

- To concede (e.g., although this may be true, granted, of course).

- To conclude or summarize (e.g., consequently, in short, finally).

- To add a point (e.g., in addition, above all, equally important).

- To compare (e.g., similarly, analogous to, likewise).

- To contrast (e.g., on the other hand, dissimilar to, a striking difference).

- To indicate cause and effect (e.g., therefore, consequently, because of, as a result of).

- To divide or classify (e.g., one part of, another category, to divide further, together with).

- To indicate spatial arrangement (e.g., near, to the left, beneath, in the foreground).

- To emphasize or intensify (e.g., even more important, the most significant, most important of all).

- To connect clauses (e.g., and, or, for, but, not only...but also, although, however, whichever).

2 – Pronoun Reference

Pronouns are words that substitute for nouns. Examples include: I, you, he, she, it, we, they, me, mine, yours, his, hers, ours, and theirs. Pronoun reference is used to show relationships within a sentence or paragraph, to avoid repeating nouns, and to provide flexibility. For example, compare, "Maria is very tired, so Maria is going to bed in Maria's room down the hall," with, "Maria is very tired, so she is going to bed in her room down the hall." Both sentences convey the same information, but the first statement is stilted. The second sentence, which contains appropriate pronoun reference, reads naturally without sacrificing clarity.

Pronouns are wonderfully flexible and useful words, but they must be used carefully. Make sure your pronoun reference is clear. The most common error made by inexperienced writers is unclear pronoun reference, which means that the reader cannot be sure which noun the pronoun is supposed to replace. For example, in the sentence, "Maria and Jennifer were tired, so she went to bed," the reader does not know if Maria went to bed or if Jennifer went to bed. Another error is the simple overuse of pronouns. Every once in a while, the writer has to remind the reader of the subject's proper name.

In addition, make sure your pronouns "agree" with their antecedents (replaced nouns) in number. In other words, if a noun is singular, then the pronoun that replaces it must also be singular; if a noun is plural, then the pronoun that replaces it must also be plural. For example, in the following sentence, the pronoun *their* "agrees with" the word "girls" to which it refers. "The *girls* forgot to bring *their* books to biology class."

3 – Repeat Key Words

Repeat key words to emphasize or reinforce ideas, but not so much that your writing becomes redundant. For example, look at the use of the word "relate" in the second paragraph of this chapter. Coherence is all about establishing relationships among sentences, and the word "relate" keeps the reader focused on that idea.

4 – Repeat Key Phrases and Clauses

Repeating a key phrase or clause in a paragraph can be an effective way to emphasize a particularly important point. Because paragraphs are relatively short, you should be careful not to repeat a key phrase too often, as that will make your writing redundant. One method is to use the key phrase twice, once in your topic sentence, and then a second time at the end of the paragraph to provide closure.

5 – Word Substitution

Properly used, word substitutions can add variety, nuance, and shades of meaning to your paragraphs. If misused, however, word substitution can cause needless confusion. A poorly chosen or inaccurate substitution can leave the reader wondering whether the substitute is a synonym for the first word or an entirely new concept. It is generally better to be slightly repetitive but clear, instead of original and confusing.

6 – Beginning of Paragraph Transition

Use beginning of paragraph transition by writing a phrase, or even a sentence or two, that echoes an idea in a previous paragraph. Then introduce the main point of the new paragraph. This technique, which helps you shift from one point to another, is sometimes referred to as a "paragraph hook" because you are using the beginning of paragraph transition to "hook" the paragraphs together.

7 – End of Paragraph Transition

Use end of paragraph transition by writing a phrase, or even a sentence or two, to introduce briefly a new subject or a different aspect of the same subject that you will discuss in the next paragraph. This technique helps you shift smoothly from one idea to another. The key to this technique is to introduce the new subject without fully explaining it; leave the explanation for the next paragraph.

8 – The Transitional Paragraph

A final technique to achieve coherence is the transitional paragraph. Used primarily in longer works, the transitional paragraph helps the writer shift from one idea to another or to change the point of view or tone of writing. For example, if you want to change from a paragraph with a humorous tone to a paragraph with a serious tone, the transitional paragraph can act as a bridge linking the two paragraphs together. Or, instead of bridging ideas or tone, the transitional paragraph can be used to separate ideas. For example, if you want to describe two countries and want to ensure that the reader sees the differences between them, you can use a transitional paragraph to highlight where the country descriptions will differ from each other. Whether used as a bridge or a separator, the transitional paragraph helps the reader follow your train of thought as you shift ideas, point of view, or tone.

For further explanation and examples, use *A Writer's Guide to Using Eight Methods of Transition*.

PLANNING AND ORGANIZING

For some writers, planning and organizing are second nature; for most writers they are not. To save time, write more clearly and convincingly, and avoid endless rewrites, come up with a plan. Your plan can be as simple as a list of points you want to cover or as complex as a detailed outline.

Here are a few simple planning steps to follow before beginning to write:

- Know your audience. Ask yourself, "What individual or group am I writing for?" or "What are my readers' backgrounds, ages, experiences, occupations, or interests?" If you know your audience, you can tailor the words you use and the length and complexity of your sentences according to how much your readers will be able to understand what you are saying. For example, if you are writing about nutrition during pregnancy, you would write differently for first time mothers than you would for a group of obstetricians.

- Define why you are writing. Many times writers dance around a subject because they have not defined a clear purpose. Complete the following sentence for the paragraph you plan to write and you will have a good handle on the major idea you will be trying to convey: "The purpose of this paragraph is to _____." For example, "The purpose of this paragraph is to convince my employer that I am worthy of a raise." As an added bonus, a clear purpose will also help you write a good topic sentence.

- Decide upon a tone for your writing. Tone will affect both your writing style and word choice. If you were requesting a raise, you obviously would select a serious tone and not a humorous or sarcastic tone.

- Finally, decide how you want to organize your paragraph. To use the same example, if you were requesting a raise, would it be better (1) to use comparison to show how you have performed your responsibilities beyond the level of expectation stated in your job description or (2) to use climactic order, presenting your reasons from the least to the most important to explain why you are worthy of a raise? Both are appropriate and can be effective, but they are quite different and you should choose before beginning to write. The remainder of this book is devoted to giving you options of how to organize your thoughts into a paragraph.

Whether you are a novice writer or one who has been writing for many years, this simple four-step plan will result in more focused writing. Good planning and good writing go hand in hand.

30 WAYS
TO WRITE PARAGRAPHS

Chronological
Descriptive
Definition
Spatial
Physical Analysis
Process Analysis
Example
Analogy
Division
Classification
Enumerative
Comparison
Contrast
Comparison and Contrast
Climactic

Anticlimactic
General to Particular
Particular to General
Simple to Complex
Opinion and Reason
Question and Answer
Problem and Solution
Cause and Effect
Dialogue
Narrative
Anecdotal
Introductory
Transitional
Concluding
Summary

WRITING A CHRONOLOGICAL PARAGRAPH

One of the most common ways to organize ideas is to put them in chronological order. You probably wrote your first chronological sequence paragraphs in elementary school when you wrote about what you did during summer break or when you wrote about a class field trip. Chronological sequence paragraphs are also used by people in the workforce. Police officers use it to write reports, journalists use it to write news stories, and nurses use it to keep daily logs of their patients.

Chronological sequence is a way of structuring and developing ideas in time order. It answers the questions: "What happened? What happened next? Then what happened?" or "What is the first step? What is the next step?"

Chronological sequence is useful for telling short stories, explaining how to make or do something, showing the origin and development of an organization, tracing historical events, presenting biographical information, or writing about personal experiences and observations.

The secret to writing a good chronological sequence paragraph lies in making sure that all events, steps, descriptions, or elements of a story are placed in correct order. If you break up the sequence or leave out a step or event, you will confuse your reader.

Example

Many of the racial and ethnic groups that live in the Hawaiian Islands today arrived at different times to work as contract laborers on the sugar and pineapple plantations. This process began in the 1850s, when the first groups of Chinese laborers arrived. The Japanese followed in the 1880s, also conscripted to work on the plantations. The Koreans and Filipinos, who began arriving in the early 1900s, were the last major Asian immigrants to the islands. The immigration process continues today, but now many of the agricultural workers arrive from Mexico and Central America.

Analysis

- The topic sentence sets the stage for the paragraph. The reader learns that the paragraph will discuss immigrants who originally came to Hawai'i to work on agricultural plantations. The reader also learns that the paragraph will be structured in time order.

- Each group is presented chronologically in order of arrival to Hawai'i.

- The paragraph has unity. All of the sentences "stick to" the main idea presented in the topic sentence. (See *Unity*).

- By using the transition "today," the final sentence takes the reader from past to present. (See *Coherence*).

Practical Suggestions

- Carefully select your beginning and ending points; they frame your paragraph and must provide logical beginnings and endings.

- If you are describing a time period, use a common measure of time; begin with the first day, month, year, decade, or century, and proceed to the next day, month, year, decade, or century.

- If you are describing events in a person's life, choose important milestones as your framework. The easiest milestones to use as your framework are birth and death, but other useful milestones include the beginning of school, graduation, marriage, or the birth of your first child or grandchild.

- When tracing a process step by step from beginning to end, you do not need to provide exact time references, but you should begin with the first event and end with the last.

- A more advanced chronological paragraph can begin with the result of an experience or event, followed by describing it using a flashback pattern (5, 1, 2, 3, 4). Many fiction writers and screenwriters use this technique.

- Use transitional words and phrases such as first, next, after that, finally, as soon as, earlier, later, or subsequently to guide the reader through the sequence of events.

WRITING A DESCRIPTIVE PARAGRAPH

A descriptive paragraph is exactly what its name implies—a paragraph that describes something. In a descriptive paragraph, writers depend on the five senses—sight, sound, touch, smell, and taste—to convey a clear, complete, and vivid description of a person, place, or thing.

Description can be used in different ways, such as to define a term (e.g., democracy, traffic jam), to explain a process in a series of steps (e.g., recipe), to locate a place (e.g., restaurant near a town square, house on a hill), or to provide insights about a person (e.g., inflexible posture and expression).

A good descriptive paragraph can be compared to a beautiful painting. Like the many colors, lines, and shapes artists paint on canvas to create clear pictures, writers create particular images or feelings with words. Readers translate these words into visual, dynamic pictures in their minds.

A descriptive paragraph can serve as a good introduction to a longer piece of writing. After describing the subject matter, the writer can then discuss various aspects of the subject in subsequent paragraphs.

Example

The Galleria in Milan, Italy, is a glass-domed arcade bustling with shops, restaurants, and one small café specializing in extraordinary coffee. I spent an afternoon relaxing in this tiny oasis, where the owners roasted batches of rich, dark brown beans right on the premises. The sound of frothing milk and the sweet aroma of brewing espresso inspired me to try many different types of coffee. My favorite was the Puglia blend, which had a fresh, nutty taste. The espresso was served in a delicate demitasse cup and topped with a small, light brown ring of foam. By the end of my visit to Italy, I came to a surprising conclusion: this tiny café tucked away in the corner of the Galleria served up the best coffee I had ever tasted.

Analysis

- The topic sentence quickly sets the stage (Milan, Italy) and then narrows the focus to the topic of the paragraph (coffee). (See *Topic Sentence*).

- The paragraph paints a picture using details based on sight, sound, smell, and taste.

- The description attempts to bring the feel of the small Italian café to the reader.

Practical Suggestions

- To help your reader form a vivid mental image of the subject, use as many of the five senses as possible.

- If you are writing about an object and are having difficulty describing it, find the object or get a picture to use as the basis of your description. Turn the visual object into a word picture.

- Know your audience. The less your readers know about the subject, the more background and detail you will need to provide. For example, if you are writing for a gourmet cooking magazine, the phrase "bok choy" might be sufficient for the reader (a gourmet chef) to form a correct mental image. If you are writing a cooking article for a general purpose magazine, on the other hand, you would need to describe the shape, size, color, taste, and texture of the vegetable in addition to where the reader would be able to find it.

- Description can help provide details of how two objects are similar or different from one another. (See *Writing a Comparison and Contrast Paragraph*).

- Descriptive paragraphs are well suited for any physical object (See *Writing a Spatial Paragraph* and *Writing a Physical Analysis Paragraph*), but they can also be useful in giving directions or in explaining a "how to" process. (See *Writing a Process Analysis Paragraph*).

WRITING A PARAGRAPH USING DEFINITION

A definition explains what a word or phrase means. Writers of every type define words and phrases to allow readers to understand a subject better.

Defining a word or phrase is a three-part process. First, the writer identifies the word or phrase being defined. Second, the writer puts the word or phrase into its proper class or category (called the "genus"). Third, the writer explains those characteristics that make the word or phrase different from other words or phrases in its class (called the "differentiae").

Note the three parts in this example: "A cellular telephone (phrase being defined) is a wireless communication device (genus), that allows people to take their phone with them and make telephone calls from practically anywhere (differences from regular phones).

While all definitions share these three basic features, there are numerous types of definitions that differ in appearance and purpose. The five most common types of definitions are: (1) single definition; (2) multiple definition; (3) definition using comparison and contrast; (4) operational definition; and (5) extended definition.

A single definition is the definition of a word or phrase by itself. A single definition paragraph is used for relatively simple terms. It is generally brief, often only two or three sentences long.

A multiple definition provides a definition of two or more terms. If the terms are relatively simple, a multiple definition paragraph can be just a few sentences, one or two for each term. For more complex terms, the paragraph can be longer or you may have to use two paragraphs.

A definition using comparison and contrast is a specific type of multiple definition in which the writer compares the similarities and contrasts the differences between two terms. Sometimes, the writer compares and contrasts a familiar, known term with an unfamiliar term the writer wishes to explain to the reader; other times, the writer uses comparison and contrast to explain two unknown terms. There are several different forms of comparison and contrast paragraphs, and the writer can use any one of these forms for a definition paragraph. (See *Writing a Comparison and Contrast Paragraph*).

An operational definition explains how something works. It can be a short paragraph (how to "rake"), a longer paragraph (how to "prune"), or a longer piece of writing (how to "landscape"). It is often written in the form of a "process analysis" paragraph. (See *Writing a Process Analysis Paragraph*).

An extended definition is a lengthier, more detailed, and very specific explanation of one or more terms. Writers can use the single, multiple, comparison and contrast, or operational definition as part of an extended definition. Often, the term being defined is quite complex. For instance, defining the nature of friendship would require an extended definition.

Example

A slave is a person who is owned by another human being, and a prisoner is a person who is detained by society. In each case, the individual is controlled by someone else and lacks personal freedoms such as the right to travel, the right to choose an occupation, and the right to choose what to do and when to do it. When these freedoms are taken away through slavery, it is universally condemned as wrong. When, however, society takes away the freedoms of a criminal through imprisonment, the action is viewed as an acceptable and necessary part of punishment and protection.

Analysis

- The example uses a multiple definition of a slave and a prisoner. The writer names the two words being defined and places each in a class (person). The writer then follows up with details showing how the slave and prisoner are different from each other and from other words in their class.

- Note how the paragraph maintains a parallel structure. That is, the topic sentence introduces "slave," then "prisoner." The analysis follows this pattern, which assists the reader in following the explanation.

Practical Suggestions

- Remember to include the name of the word, the class or category to which it belongs, and how or why it is different from others in its category.

- Do not use a form of the word being defined in the definition. For example, do not write "Democracy is a democratic form of government." The one possible exception to this rule is when the phrase being defined is a subset of a common item. For instance, it may be proper to use the word "telephone" within the definition of a "cellular telephone."

- Definitions are not always objective. There are hundreds of definitions of love, for example. In some cases, you can define terms according to your own perception of the term based on personal experience and observation.

- Avoid saying, "According to the dictionary..." to define a word. This is a tired and overused phrase. When you do use the dictionary, however, follow the rules of research writing by documenting the source.

- Definition is well suited to division, where the whole (the subject word or phrase) is divided into its component parts, and each part is discussed one point at a time. (See *Writing a Paragraph Using Division*).

WRITING A SPATIAL PARAGRAPH

A spatial paragraph is used to describe the location and physical attributes of a place, thing, or even a person. Writers use the spatial method of organizing when they need to arrange and analyze things that are physical, such as land areas (countries, cities, parks), bodies of water, buildings, and human anatomy.

To write a spatial paragraph, first choose a descriptive approach; that is, decide how you will describe the subject. Will you describe it from one direction to another (top to bottom, north to south, river source to river mouth, head to toe), by theme (mountain ranges, rivers, types of organs), by a map view (locating nearby countries, referring to the general shape of a country), or by a combination of methods? Each of these approaches can be effective, but it is important to pick an overall approach so the reader can follow your logic. Feel free to use a variety of descriptive words from several different approaches, but make sure your reader is taken along one basic "path."

Once you have chosen an approach, your next goal is to paint a clear picture of the subject for the reader. To move from point to point and describe how things relate to each other, use spatial transitional words and expressions (e.g., above, below, at the base of, on the opposite side, in the background, to the left, on the right).

The spatial method of arranging ideas is an excellent organizational tool for a wide variety of fields, including science and technology, sports, architecture, engineering, apparel design, geography, surveying, home decorating, city planning, and medicine.

Example

Italy is a southern European country defined by mountains and sea. It is composed of a long, narrow peninsula, the three major islands of Sicily, Sardinia and Elba, and many smaller islands. Italy is easily found on a map because it is shaped like a high-heeled boot. The top of the boot is formed by the main peninsula, the heel and toe are formed by smaller peninsulas, and the boot looks like it is kicking the island of Sicily to the west. Italy's northern border is bounded by the rugged Alps, which it shares with France, Switzerland, Austria, and Slovenia. The rest of Italy, and by far the majority, is surrounded by water. To the west and south lies the Mediterranean Sea, and to the east lies the Adriatic Sea.

Analysis

- The paragraph focuses on a geographic description of Italy using a map view approach. The writer helps the reader understand the location of the country by showing its relationships to land and sea using descriptive and directional words (northern border, west, east, surrounded).

- The paragraph begins by dividing Italy by land and water. The two subjects are then presented in the order in which they were first listed: land first and water second. (See *Writing an Enumerative Paragraph*).

- The writer uses a word picture ("high-heeled boot") to help the reader visualize the shape of Italy. This word picture creates a clear physical description. The reader should have no difficulty locating Italy on a map of Europe.

Practical Suggestions

- A good approach to writing a spatial paragraph is to place a picture of the subject you wish to explain in front of you. If a picture is unavailable, try to draw one before beginning to write. You can then use the picture to guide your writing.

- If you or a friend can visualize or draw the object, picture, or design you have described in your spatial paragraph, you have a successful piece of writing. If you cannot visualize or draw the subject, go back and revise your paragraph to achieve greater clarity.

- For descriptions that require detailed information, write for an audience you assume used to be sighted, but is now blind. In that way, you can create exacting mental pictures for your readers.

WRITING
A PHYSICAL ANALYSIS
PARAGRAPH

A physical analysis paragraph answers the question, "What does it look like?" Description is an important element of a good physical analysis paragraph. A physical analysis paragraph incorporates as many of the five senses as necessary to provide a full understanding of the subject. (See *Writing a Descriptive Paragraph*).

Conceptually, a physical analysis paragraph can be quite similar to a spatial paragraph. Organizationally, a physical analysis paragraph can be quite similar to a division paragraph.

First, like a spatial paragraph, a physical analysis paragraph focuses on a physical object or objects taking up space. For example, a writer can use a physical analysis paragraph to describe a person, such as a character in a story; a place, such as Mt. St. Helens; or a thing, such as a digital camera. (See *Writing a Spatial Paragraph*).

The difference between spatial and physical analysis paragraphs is that spatial paragraphs are limited to how objects are situated in space, whereas physical analysis paragraphs also describe the specific attributes of the object. For example, in describing the mountains of northern Italy, a spatial paragraph might state that the mountains form the northern border of Italy and run generally east to west, whereas a physical analysis paragraph might also include the facts that the mountains are extremely rugged, are composed largely of limestone, and have some of the best ski areas in the world tucked into their high valleys.

Second, a physical analysis paragraph generally uses division as an organizing theme. In other words, the whole is divided into its parts and then each part is described piece by piece. For example, a writer can provide a physical analysis of a river by dividing it into three parts—the tributaries, the main stem, and the mouth—and then discussing each part. (See *Writing a Paragraph Using Division*).

Example

One of the many features that entices visitors to Hawai'i is the opportunity to see an active volcano. Kilauea, on the Big Island of Hawai'i, has been erupting continuously for almost two decades. Perhaps Kilauea's most exciting and popular attraction is Halema'uma'u, which is a volcanic caldera, or crater, sitting atop one of Kilauea's most active vents. Visitors are first surprised at the sheer size of Halema'uma'u, which is almost 300 feet deep and spans two miles from rim to rim. The caldera resembles a large round lake, except that it occasionally is filled with boiling lava, not cool water. Currently, the molten lava is covered by a crust of hardened lava, but at other times the surface has been a seething mass of orange-red liquid lava. Around and inside the pit, pungent sulfur gases seep through small vents in the lava rock formations. Visitors stand on the crater rim in awe of the size and power of this sight.

Analysis

- The paragraph provides a physical description of Halemaʻumaʻu, one part of the Kilauea volcano complex. Rather than attempting to describe the entire volcano, which would require multiple paragraphs, the writer instead focuses on one feature that can be described in a single paragraph.

- The physical analysis breaks the caldera down into component parts: size, shape, color, appearance, smell, and effect on observers.

- Note how the writer uses two introductory sentences to bring the reader from a general idea of visiting Hawaiian volcanoes to a description of an exciting feature of one volcano.

Practical Suggestions

- To determine if a subject is suitable for a physical analysis paragraph, ask the question, "Can I see it?" If the answer is "yes," a physical analysis paragraph is appropriate.

- Use physical analysis paragraphs for geography and geographical features, the sciences, visual arts, and medicine. Professionals who use physical analysis include architects, engineers, city planners, interior designers, doctors, veterinarians, and investigators.

- A physical analysis paragraph should be as detailed as possible to create a picture in the reader's mind. Use vivid words and phrases. To prevent your physical analysis paragraph from becoming too long, choose every sentence carefully. Avoid sentences that do not really advance the main idea of your paragraph.

WRITING
A PROCESS ANALYSIS
PARAGRAPH

Writing a process analysis paragraph involves explaining how something works or instructing how to do something. All "how to" books, including this one, are filled with explanations that use the process analysis method. The goal of a process analysis paragraph is to take the reader through the process being described, explaining each step along the way.

The organization of process analysis paragraphs is similar to that of enumeration paragraphs. The whole is divided into its component parts, and then each part is explained piece by piece and step by step. For example, a writer might begin: "There are seven simple steps to changing a flat tire. First,... Second,...." (See *Writing an Enumerative Paragraph*). This organization is also quite similar to paragraphs using division and time sequence. (See *Writing a Paragraph Using Division* and *Writing a Chronological Paragraph*).

A good test for clear and concise process analysis writing is to have someone else read and check your writing for clarity. The reader should not only be able to follow the process step by step, but also be able to explain the process back to you in his or her own words.

As is true for all writing, the key to good process analysis writing is to know your audience. For example, a paragraph explaining how to install a new computer program would be quite different if it were written for a group of people who have little familiarity with computers than if it were written for a group of computer buffs. (See *Planning and Organizing*).

Process analysis writing is used by a wide group of writers known as technical writers. These are the people who write assembly and use instructions for toys, computers, furniture, and countless other products. Anyone who has struggled to put together a toy using poor instructions will recognize the importance of good process analysis writing.

Example

Deciding how to resolve disputes is an age-old dilemma throughout the world. One solution, used by children in nearly every country, is a simple hand game known in various languages as "Jan Ken Po," "Ching Chong Chow," "Ro Sham Bo," and "Rock Paper Scissors." Regardless of its name, the rules are the same. Two players face each other, extend one forearm, and make a fist. The players then move their fists up and down three times, calling out at the bottom of each movement one of the syllables of the name (in their own language) or counting to three. On the third downward move, the players each "show" a hand symbol of a rock, paper, or scissors. A rock is shown by a fist, paper is shown by extending the fingers and holding the hand horizontally, and scissors is shown by extending and spreading the index and middle fingers. If both players show the same symbol, then the game is a tie and is replayed. If the players show different symbols, then there will be a winner: rock smashes (and beats) scissors; scissors cuts (and beats) paper; and paper covers (and beats) rock.

Analysis

- The paragraph provides step-by-step directions for a game played throughout the world to solve disputes.

- The paragraph is organized into a series of chronological steps. (See *Writing a Chronological Paragraph*).

- The writer begins by posing a universal problem of solving disputes, and then provides a solution in the form of a game. The problem and solution paragraph is therefore an appropriate method of organizing a process analysis paragraph. (See *Writing a Problem and Solution Paragraph*).

Practical Suggestions

- Before you begin writing, list each step in the process you are describing. If necessary, actually go through the process yourself to make sure you do not miss any steps. For example, if you are writing about how to use a DVD player, go through the steps using your own player and write down each step as you go along. (See *Planning and Organizing*).

- Although it is important to explain each step clearly, do not oversimplify the process so much that you bore or even insult your reader.

- Sometimes complex processes need not only written steps, but also visual aids such as charts, diagrams, or pictures. A careful analysis of your subject and audience will help you determine whether or not to include visual aids.

WRITING AN EXAMPLE PARAGRAPH

You have probably heard the phrase, "A picture is worth a thousand words." An example paragraph is the written manifestation of that phrase. Writers commonly use example paragraphs to explain complex situations and concepts and to add life to their writing. When done successfully, an example paragraph can take a long, rambling, complicated, theoretical concept and explain it through a short, concise, easily understood, real-world illustration.

The main goal of an example paragraph is to provide one illustration of the concept you are trying to explain and, by that illustration, help the reader understand the entire concept. An effective way to accomplish this goal is to provide the conceptual explanation first, and then show how the concept works in the real world through an example.

There are as many examples as there are concepts, so there is no single rule for developing an example paragraph, but here are some ideas to keep in mind. First, make sure your example actually illustrates the concept you are explaining. If you are trying to explain the steepness of mountains, but provide examples about the height of mountains, the reader will be confused. Second, try to use examples that the reader will understand. The reader will be much more able to concentrate on the difficult concept you are trying to illustrate if the words, places, and language used in the example are already familiar.

There are three ways to organize a paragraph using examples: (1) single example; (2) multiple example; and (3) hypothetical example. The single example is simply what its name suggests. One example is provided. For instance, to explain activism among college students, a writer can select one student that best represents a group of proactive students. If additional clarification of the variety of campus activism is necessary, a writer can use a multiple example, such as a male freshman and a female senior. When no real, specific example is available, a writer can use a "made up" or hypothetical example. The writer invents an example that best represents the larger subject even though it may not have a basis in real life. Hypothetical examples can also be either single or multiple in their development.

Example: Single

In Hawai'i, the mountains, valleys, and even people's backyards contain many natural medicinal plants that are no longer used, or even known, by most people. One example is the kukui nut. Simply pick some of the fresh nuts and press them to remove the oil. Used sparingly, the oil is a natural, safe laxative.

Example: Multiple

In Hawai'i, the mountains, valleys, and even people's backyards contain many natural medicinal plants that are no longer used, or even known, by most people. One example is the kukui nut. Simply pick some of the fresh nuts and press them to remove the oil. Used sparingly, the oil is a natural, safe laxative. Another illustration is the guava leaf, which has the opposite effect of the kukui nut. Pick a few small budding leaves at the end of a guava branch; the leaves should be tiny, tender, and a translucent, light green color. Wash the leaves, chew them well, and swallow. Use this remedy to stop diarrhea.

Example: Hypothetical

In Hawai'i and other Polynesian islands, the mountains, valleys, and even people's backyards contain many natural medicinal plants that are no longer used, or even known, by most people. If a Native Hawaiian familiar with the medicinal qualities of local plants and a European traveler unfamiliar with those qualities were each stranded on a deserted Polynesian island, there is little doubt who would fare better. The European would be subject to the pains and inconveniences of common but seemingly uncontrollable illnesses. However, the Native Hawaiian, with his knowledge of natural, medicinal plants—such as kukui nuts as laxatives and guava leaves as anti-diuretics—would be better able to fend off the common, debilitating illnesses and concentrate on the major tasks of obtaining food and shelter.

Analysis

- The single example extracts one part from the whole, the kukui nut as a natural laxative. The message to the reader is simply that natural remedies exist.

- The multiple example extracts two parts from the whole, kukui nuts and guava leaves. These plants have opposite medicinal effects, so the message to the reader is more complex: there are a variety of natural medicines that can remedy a variety of ailments.

- The hypothetical or "what if" example provides an even more complex level of analysis. By introducing hypothetical characters into the example, the writer conveys not only that there are a number of natural remedies, but also that knowledge of natural remedies can have advantages.

- All three illustrations use transitional words and expressions (one example, another illustration, however). (See *Coherence*).

Practical Suggestions

- The purpose of providing examples is to make it easier to understand a subject. Be sure the example represents the subject as a whole. If not, the paragraph may confuse or not convince the reader of your idea.

- Draw a circle and label it with your subject. Within the circle, list specific examples of your subject. Decide whether a single example will suffice, or whether you will need to use a multiple or hypothetical example to fully explain your subject.

- Example paragraphs can follow one of several different paragraph structures. Single examples often follow the general to particular structure. (See *Writing a General to Particular Paragraph*).

Multiple examples can follow either the comparison and contrast structure or the enumerative model. (See *Writing a Comparison and Contrast Paragraph* and *Writing an Enumerative Paragraph*).

WRITING
A PARAGRAPH USING
ANALOGY

An analogy is a method used by writers to explain an unfamiliar, often complex concept in terms that are familiar to the audience. Technically, an analogy is a comparison of subjects that are generally dissimilar, but that share one particular feature that can help the reader understand the more complex subject. For example, a writer could describe the horrors of total warfare by analogizing it to a battle between colonies of red ants and black ants. Ants and humans obviously are not the same, but the brutality of ant battles can help the reader comprehend the savagery of total war.

Analogies share some features with both comparisons and examples, which also use one idea or concept to explain another. Like comparisons, analogies show similarities between two concepts. (See *Writing a Comparison Paragraph*). Like examples, analogies often use concrete illustrations to help explain a theoretical concept. (See *Writing an Example Paragraph*). Unlike comparisons and examples, however, the ideas and information in analogies are not from the same group or category. Instead, the ideas and information in an analogy are generally quite different and share only one feature. That one feature, however, is what the writer is using to help the reader understand.

Writing an analogy requires careful thought. The writer must be sure that the subjects are not so different that the reader cannot focus on the one, all-important shared feature. The writer must also be sure that all of the comparisons and similarities are intended; very often two subjects have more than one similarity, and the reader might not focus on the correct one.

Example

Have you ever thought what clothes would be like without buttons? Buttons come in many different shapes and sizes, but they are all connectors. They connect the two sides of our shirts, blouses, and jackets. Without buttons, a shirt would not be a shirt, and a blouse would not be a blouse; both would just be pieces of cloth with armholes. Good writing needs connectors, too, called transitions. Just as there are different shapes and sizes of buttons, there are different types of transitions to fit a variety of writing needs. Writers can use transitional words and expressions, repeat key words and phrases, use pronoun reference, or use word substitution. Buttons make our clothes fit from top to bottom, and good transitions allow readers to follow the writer's ideas from sentence to sentence and from beginning to end.

Analysis

- The writer selects a familiar subject (buttons) to explain an unfamiliar subject (transitions). Even though buttons and transitions seem quite different, the key concept of connecting is shared by both.

- The writer focuses only on one aspect of buttons, which helps the reader focus on the similarities between buttons and transitions, rather than the differences.

- The example repeats key words and phrases to establish coherence and reinforce the point of the paragraph. For example, the word "connect" or "connector" appears three times in the example, reinforcing the similarities between buttons and transitions. (See *Coherence*).

Practical Suggestions

- Know your audience. Make sure your audience understands and is familiar with your "known" subject. To use the example from the beginning of this chapter, it would be unwise to explain the brutality of war by analogizing to red and black ants if your audience has no familiarity with the violence of a battle between ant colonies.

- Analogies are particularly useful to explain abstract, complex, obscure, or unfamiliar concepts.

- An analogy can be an effective opening paragraph for a composition because the writer can use the analogy to intrigue the reader about the actual subject.

- An analogy frequently includes two or more unlike but familiar subjects that are used to explain an unfamiliar subject. To build on the earlier example, ants and bees (insects commonly known for group effort and industriousness) may be used to describe an Israeli kibbutz or a successful commune (unfamiliar concepts).

WRITING A PARAGRAPH USING DIVISION

Division is a method of taking a whole subject and dividing it into its component parts. Writing a division paragraph is like emptying items from a basket full of related goods. Remove the items one at a time and write about each item as it relates to the whole subject.

A division paragraph differs from other similar types of paragraphs because all items in a division paragraph must fall into the same class, group, or category. For example, it would be appropriate to use a division paragraph to discuss a basket of apples, tangerines, and kiwi, which are all fruits, but it would require a different type of paragraph if the writer added lettuce and beans to the basket. (See *Writing a General to Particular Paragraph*, *Writing an Enumerative Paragraph*, and *Writing a Comparison and Contrast Paragraph*).

When writing a division paragraph, first state the subject and then divide it into its parts. Discuss each part in the same order in which it was named.

Division is an excellent way to organize ideas because the subject is explored in bite-sized pieces. Not only is it easier for the writer to explain a subject piece by piece, but it is also easier for the reader to understand a subject when it is presented in small parts.

People who use division paragraphs include travel writers, chefs, sociologists, fashion writers, and astronomers. These are all people who study or work with subjects that are related to each other. For example, a travel writer would use division to discuss topics such as the spectacular geysers in Yellowstone National Park, while a chef may use division to write about the different types of apples grown in Washington.

Example

Although immortality remains a myth, the increasing life span of Americans is shattering traditional ideas about human longevity. As of the year 2000, people age eighty-five and older are the fastest growing segment of the population. Doctors recommend regular exercise, a nutritious diet, and a low-stress lifestyle as three factors contributing to longevity. Regular exercise three to four times a week, such as walking, running, or cycling, keeps the heart, lungs, and mind strong. A healthy, nutritious diet that includes proteins, fruits, vegetables, and whole grains helps to control weight and maintain energy levels. A lifestyle that reduces stress, unnecessary tension, and anger can reduce blood pressure and may prevent heart problems. Follow these three recommendations and you not only might make it to eighty-five, but also might join the growing number of centenarians, already almost 100,000 strong as of 2000, and expected to grow to 834,000 by 2050.

Analysis

- The writer selects recommendations for longevity as the category or group, divides the group into three parts (exercise, diet, and lifestyle), and briefly discusses each part.

- Note how the third sentence provides "organizational clues" to how the writer will discuss the parts. The writer then discusses the parts in the same order they were introduced.

- The writer enlivens a relatively mundane topic (the three keys to longevity) in the first and last sentences. The first sentence uses the myth of immortality to introduce the topic. The last sentence uses statistics to show that the three keys to longevity can make reaching 100 years of age a real possibility in today's world.

Practical Suggestions

- Note the similarity between ideas developed by division paragraphs, enumeration paragraphs, and general to particular paragraphs. (See *Writing an Enumerative Paragraph* and *Writing a General to Particular Paragraph*).

- Many of the keys to a successful division paragraph are also used for enumerative paragraphs and general to particular paragraphs: select a topic that is clear and divides easily; make sure the parts relate to the topic sentence; use consistent organization; and ensure that the entire paragraph relates to one common idea or category.

- If one part is more important than another, it is often effective to state the parts from the least important to the most important for a climactically organized paragraph. (See *Writing a Climactic Paragraph*).

- Outlining is particularly effective in organizing a division paragraph. After outlining a main topic and its supporting points, converting the outline into a division paragraph is a natural next step.

WRITING
A PARAGRAPH USING
CLASSIFICATION

Classification involves discussing the separate parts of a subject individually to reach an understanding of the whole subject. Classification is similar to division. Both are ways of organizing ideas according to their component parts. (See *Writing a Paragraph Using Division*).

Visually, classification can be viewed as putting items into a basket and then concluding with an explanation of what the basket contains. In contrast, division involves identifying the basket first, and then emptying the items out and writing about each item as it is removed. In essence, division and classification involve the same concept, but are approached from opposite sides.

Because of their similarities, classification and division share similar requirements. Both require that all parts relate to the whole and be from the same group or category. When writing about fruits, for example, foods from another group such as vegetables should not be included unless the writer is comparing or contrasting the two groups. (See *Writing a Comparison and Contrast Paragraph*).

Classification, like division, is a good way to organize ideas into bite-sized pieces. Not only is it easier for the writer to explain a subject piece by piece, but it is also easier for the reader to follow the subject one piece at a time.

Classification paragraphs also share some similarities with simple to complex paragraphs. Both involve building up to the final broad topic by discussing its component parts. Classification paragraphs differ from simple to complex paragraphs, however, because classification paragraphs require that the component parts be from the same class of subjects while simple to complex paragraphs can include a wide variety of parts, including parts from different categories. (See *Writing a Simple to Complex Paragraph*).

Example

Hawai'i offers examples of three classifications of plants. First, endemic plants are plants that exist in a specific location and nowhere else. Because of their isolation, the Hawaiian islands have a great number of endemic plants. Endemic plants in Hawai'i originally arrived from other parts of the world by wind, sea, and birds, but over time they changed so much that they are now recognized as independent species. Second, indigenous plants are native to a particular area, but also grow in other locations. For example, many of the palm trees in Hawai'i are also found throughout the South Pacific, so they are defined as indigenous plants. Finally, alien or exotic plants are ones that arrive in a particular place only with human help. In Hawai'i, the initial group of alien plant species arrived when the Native Hawaiians brought plants with them from other Pacific Islands. For the most part, these plants were able to coexist with the existing endemic and indigenous plants. A later group of alien plant species began arriving when Europeans first visited the Hawaiian islands. This later group of alien plants has been much more destructive to the endemic and indigenous species than the plants brought by Native Hawaiians. In fact, these later alien plants have endangered many of the endemic and indigenous plants, as well as plants introduced by Native Hawaiians. Today, there is a great effort to preserve the endemic and indigenous plants of Hawai'i.

Analysis

- The writer discusses three ways in which plants are classified (endemic, indigenous, and alien), and then discusses how each relates to the larger category of Hawaiian plants.

- The paragraph is unified because all of the sentences in the paragraph relate to the main idea stated in the topic sentence. (See *Unity*).

- The writer maintains coherence by tying sentences together using transitional words and phrases (first, second, finally, for example, today). (See *Coherence*).

- The writer embeds other methods of organizing ideas, including comparison, contrast, and definition. (See *Writing a Comparison and Contrast Paragraph* and *Writing a Definition Paragraph*).

Practical Suggestions

- Think of classification as a process that begins with a broad subject and moves to specific subjects that are included within the broad subjects. (See *Writing a General to Particular Paragraph*).

- Classification can be used for almost any subject, particularly because persons, places, and objects fall into many different categories.

- Classification is commonly used in scientific writing. The example above shows how a botanist would use classification to discuss the plants of Hawaiʻi.

WRITING
AN ENUMERATIVE
PARAGRAPH

Enumeration is one of the most common and practical ways to organize a paragraph. If a subject can be divided into separate parts that can be numbered and discussed, then the enumerative paragraph structure is ideal.

In an enumerative paragraph, the writer first states the subject in the topic sentence. Next, the writer divides the subject into its component parts and introduces each part. Then, the writer discusses each part in the order in which it was named, using numerical transitions (e.g., first, second, third). Enumerative paragraphs are quite similar to division paragraphs, with the primary difference being that enumerative paragraphs specifically number the parts being discussed.

The component parts of an enumerative paragraph can be organized in a variety of ways. One of the most common is chronological, where the writer discusses the parts in the order they occurred. (See *Writing a Chronological Paragraph*). Other logical choices include climactic, anticlimactic, general to particular, and particular to general. (See *Writing a Climactic Paragraph*, *Writing an Anticlimactic Paragraph*, *Writing a General to Particular Paragraph*, and *Writing a Particular to General Paragraph*). Ultimately, the writer must choose the order that makes the most sense for a particular subject.

Example

The Chinese civilization is more than three thousand years old, and its people have maintained many of their cultural traditions for generations. Three Chinese traditions, however, have changed dramatically in the last century: the role of husbands, the practice of arranged marriages, and the role of women in society. First, husbands no longer have absolute control over their wives and families. Husbands increasingly share decisionmaking with their wives. Second, arranged marriages are now quite rare, as most Chinese favor marrying someone based on love. Traditional arranged marriages focused more on social status and economic factors, which are not as important to young people in modern China. Third, women have dramatically increased their roles in Chinese society. Women in China today are much more likely than in times past to pursue lifelong careers, travel abroad, and have fewer children.

Analysis

- The paragraph enumerates three ways Chinese traditions have changed. The writer first introduces the subject, next divides it into three parts, and then discusses the parts in order.

- The writer uses numerical transitions: first, second, and third.

- In this paragraph, there is no clearly preferable order for the component parts. They are not chronological events, all are important changes, and no one part is plainly more important than another. Given these circumstances, the writer simply chose an order that could be written about fairly easily: men's roles as husbands, how men and women choose to marry, and women's roles in society.

- To write a longer and more fully developed composition based on this example, subsequent paragraphs could expand on the parts enumerated in the initial paragraph. The topic sentence for the next paragraph would include the "role of husbands," the topic sentence for the following paragraph would include "arranged marriages," and the topic sentence for the last paragraph would include "women's roles." (See *Organizing Multiple Paragraphs*).

Practical Suggestions

- When a subject is complex, breaking it down into parts makes writing about it easier and reading about it more understandable. Bite-sized pieces make good sense for both writer and reader.

- Make sure you write about the subjects in the order they are introduced. Changing the order in the paragraph will confuse your reader.

- As a general guide, do not divide your subject into more than five parts. Any more parts within a single paragraph will confuse your reader. If more parts are needed, consider writing a longer composition with each part in a separate paragraph.

- Enumerative paragraphs are a good way to present structured arguments, reasons, solutions to a problem, or parts of a complex subject.

WRITING A COMPARISON PARAGRAPH

Comparison is the process of writing about how things are alike. A comparison paragraph centers on developing the similarities between subjects. The similarities can come in a variety of forms: shape, size, color, use, taste, smell, and countless others. It is natural to wonder how things are alike, and a comparison paragraph responds to that question.

Writing a comparison paragraph is relatively straightforward. First, decide which aspects of the subjects to compare (e.g., size, color, shape, use). Next, write down how the aspects of each subject are similar. Finally, choose how best to organize these similarities and begin writing.

Two common methods of organizing comparison paragraphs are the climactic and anticlimactic methods. In the climactic method, start with the similarity that is the least important to the story or idea you are developing and work up to the similarity that is most important. (See *Writing a Climactic Paragraph*). In the anticlimactic paragraph, the organization is reversed; start with the most important similarity and end with the least important. (See *Writing an Anticlimactic Paragraph*).

Example

Despite being separated by thousands of miles of ocean, Alaska and Hawai'i share some remarkable similarities. Historically, Alaska and Hawai'i were the last two states to join the United States. In addition, both are geographically separated from the other 48 states; Alaska is separated from the "Lower 48" by another country (Canada), and Hawai'i is separated from the "Mainland" by the Pacific Ocean. They are also blessed with exceptional natural beauty and draw visitors from around the world. Finally, both states have significant native populations that continue to play important roles in modern society and culture.

Analysis

- The topic sentence tells the reader that the paragraph will be about the similarities between Alaska and Hawai'i. (See *Topic Sentence*). Each example sentence "sticks to" the topic sentence. (See *Unity*).

- The writer discusses the subjects in the same order in which they were introduced: Alaska followed by Hawai'i. This format is called "parallel structure" and is one of the hallmarks of good writing.

- The writer uses transitions (in addition, also, finally) to guide the reader through the paragraph. (See *Coherence*).

- The writer uses specific examples and vivid descriptions to emphasize the similarities between the subjects.

COMPARISON

Practical Suggestions

- One way to develop a comparison paragraph is to list the similarities on a sheet of paper. The list will provide a starting point and allow you to analyze which specific aspects of the subjects you wish to compare and which organizational pattern best suits your needs.

- Comparison can involve several aspects of two subjects. For example, you can use a comparison paragraph to discuss the past, present, and future of two subjects to show how they have changed over time while still retaining certain similarities. (See *Writing a Chronological Paragraph*). A good example of this would be the relationship between men and women. Although men's and women's roles in society have certainly changed over time, there are many aspects of male-female relationships that have remained constant.

- If your subjects have differences that simply cannot be ignored, consider using a comparison and contrast paragraph. (See *Writing a Comparison and Contrast Paragraph*).

WRITING A CONTRAST PARAGRAPH

A contrast paragraph focuses on developing differences between subjects. Just as it is natural to look at how subjects are similar to one another, it is also natural to look at how subjects differ from each other. This human tendency helps us categorize the flood of information we receive every day.

Writing a contrast paragraph is quite simple and is similar to writing a comparison paragraph. First, decide which aspects of the subjects you are differentiating; are you distinguishing by size, color, shape, function, use, or some other category? Second, write down how the aspects of each subject differ. Finally, decide how to organize these differences and begin writing.

Common methods of organizing contrast paragraphs include the climactic and anticlimactic methods. The climactic method starts with the least important difference and ends with the most important difference. (See *Writing a Climactic Paragraph*). The anticlimactic method is just the reverse; it begins with the most important difference and ends with the least important difference. (See *Writing an Anticlimactic Paragraph*).

Anyone who wishes to point out the differences between two subjects can use contrast paragraphs. For example, editorial writers use contrast paragraphs to point out that two apparently similar subjects are actually different. Historians who want to emphasize the differences between presidents, governments, countries, or peoples might also use contrast paragraphs.

Example

Although they share the distinction of being the last two states to join the United States, Alaska and Hawai'i are quite different. The two most obvious differences are size and weather. Alaska is by far the largest state, being more than twice the size of any other state. Hawai'i, in contrast, is one of the smaller states, ranking forty-third in size. Alaska is quite cold, with long, dark winters and short, intense summers. Hawai'i, on the other hand, has a tropical climate and is warm throughout most of the year. A less obvious difference is the availability of natural resources. Alaska is filled with a variety of minerals and natural resources and is a major source of oil for the United States. Hawai'i, however, has relatively few natural resources and must import most of its raw materials. Finally, even the people of Alaska and Hawai'i are different. Although both have significant native populations, Alaska's immigrants have come primarily from within the United States, while Hawai'i's immigrants have come from throughout the world.

Analysis

- The topic sentence tells the reader that the paragraph will be about the differences between Alaska and Hawai'i. (See *Topic Sentence*). Each example sentence "sticks to" the topic sentence. (See *Unity*).

- The writer discusses the subjects in the same order in which they were introduced: Alaska followed by Hawai'i. This format is called "parallel structure" and is one of the hallmarks of good writing.

- The writer uses transitional words and phrases (in contrast, on the other hand, however, finally) to maintain coherence in the paragraph. (See *Coherence*).

- The writer uses concrete examples to show the differences between Alaska and Hawai'i. The reader comes away with a vivid picture of the differences between the two states rather than vague opinions that one is "prettier" or "nicer" than the other.

Practical Suggestions

- Use examples and in-depth descriptions to emphasize the differences between subjects, particularly when the differences seem small but you think they are actually quite large.

- Contrast paragraphs are effective when writing to persuade or to describe. Providing details of the differences between two subjects can help the reader understand the subjects more and may convince the reader that the two subjects should be treated differently (if that is your goal).

- An easy way to develop a subject for a contrast paragraph is to list all of the differences between two subjects on a sheet of paper, and then move those differences around until you have an organization that works for you.

- Contrast paragraphs are effective ways to express why you like one subject more than another. For instance, a writer could use a contrast paragraph to explain a preference for chocolate rather than vanilla ice cream.

- If your subjects have similarities that simply cannot be ignored, consider using a comparison and contrast paragraph. (See *Writing a Comparison and Contrast Paragraph*).

WRITING
A COMPARISON
AND CONTRAST
PARAGRAPH

Comparison is the process of writing about how things are alike, and contrast is the process of writing about how things are different. While a paragraph can be purely a comparison or purely a contrast, it is frequently more effective to combine the methods into a "comparison and contrast" paragraph. Three common structures for comparison and contrast paragraphs are: (1) the alternating pattern; (2) the block pattern; and (3) the similar-dissimilar pattern.

In the alternating pattern, the writer breaks the subjects down into their component parts, and then compares and contrasts each part before moving on to the next part. For example, if the writer is using the alternating pattern to compare and contrast two objects, the writer might first compare and contrast the colors of the two objects, then compare and contrast the size, then compare and contrast the shape, and finally compare and contrast the function of each object. This method is frequently used for short pieces of writing and can be effective in pointing out numerous, but small, variations among subjects.

Writers using the block pattern first discuss all aspects of one subject, and then discuss all aspects of the other subject or subjects. To continue the example from the previous paragraph, a writer using the block pattern to compare and contrast two objects would describe the color, size, shape, and function of the first object, and then describe the color, size, shape and function of the second object. Because this pattern keeps all parts of each subject together, the reader can better understand each subject by itself. Writers frequently use this method for longer pieces of writing.

The similar-dissimilar pattern is a particular type of block pattern in which the writer presents all of the similarities in the first block followed by all of the differences in the second block. This pattern can be effective to show that two subjects are more alike than different or more different than alike.

Example: Alternating Pattern

Alaska and Hawai'i, two states separated by thousands of miles of ocean, share some remarkable similarities and some stark differences. In size, Alaska is an extremely large state, while Hawai'i is relatively small. Both are filled with exceptional natural beauty, draw visitors from around the world, and have thriving tourist industries. Alaska's economy is much more diverse than Hawai'i's, in part because Alaska is filled with a variety of minerals and natural resources and is a major source of oil for the rest of the country. Hawai'i, in contrast, has relatively few natural resources. The people of Alaska and Hawai'i also share certain similarities and differences. Both have significant native populations, but

Alaska's immigrants have come primarily from within the United States, while Hawai'i's immigrants are from throughout the world.

Example: Block Pattern

Hawai'i and Alaska, two states separated by thousands of miles of ocean, share some remarkable similarities and some stark differences. Hawai'i is a relatively small state, but it is blessed with exceptional natural beauty and a warm, tropical climate. As a result, it has a thriving tourist economy. Unfortunately, Hawai'i has few natural resources and must import most of its raw materials. Hawai'i's people are incredibly diverse, with a significant native population mixed with immigrants from around the world. Alaska, on the other hand, is an exceptionally large state; it is by far the largest state in the United States. Like Hawai'i, Alaska is filled with exceptional natural beauty and despite its long, cold winters, it also draws visitors from around the world. Unlike Hawai'i, Alaska is filled with a variety of minerals and natural resources and is a major source of oil for the rest of the country. Finally, Alaska has a significant native population, but its immigrants come primarily from within the United States.

Example: Similar-Dissimilar Pattern

Alaska and Hawai'i, two states separated by thousands of miles of ocean, share some remarkable similarities and some stark differences. In addition to being the last two states to join the United States, Alaska and Hawai'i are blessed with exceptional natural beauty and draw visitors from around the world. Both states also have significant native populations that continue to play important roles in modern society and culture. Despite these similarities, Alaska and Hawai'i have many fundamental differences. The most obvious differences are in the states' sizes and climates. Alaska is the largest state in the country, while Hawai'i is relatively small. Alaska is also quite far north, and has long cold winters and short summers. Hawai'i, in contrast, is near the tropics, and has warm, sunny weather throughout most of the year. A less obvious difference is the availability of natural resources. Alaska is filled with a variety of minerals and natural resources and is a major source of oil for the rest of the country. Hawai'i has few natural resources and must import most of its raw materials. A final difference is in the states' immigrant population. Alaska's immigrants have come mainly from within the United States, but Hawai'i's have come from countries around the world.

Analysis

Note the organization of the three types of comparison and contrast paragraphs.

Alternating Pattern:

Size
- Alaska – large
- Hawai'i – small

Natural Beauty
- Both – beautiful

Tourism
- Both – from around the world

Natural Resources
- Alaska – many
- Hawai'i – few

Native Population
- Both – significant

Immigrant Population
- Alaska – mainly from within the United States
- Hawai'i – from all over the world

COMPARISON AND CONTRAST

Block Pattern:

Hawai'i
- Size – small
- Natural beauty – beautiful
- Climate – tropical and warm
- Tourism – from around the world
- Natural resources – few
- Native population – significant
- Immigrant population – from all over the world

Alaska
- Size – large
- Natural beauty – beautiful
- Climate – long, cold winters
- Tourism – from around the world
- Natural resources – many
- Native population – significant
- Immigrant population – mainly from within the United States

Similar-Dissimilar Pattern:

Similarities
- History – last two states to join United States
- Natural beauty – beautiful
- Tourism – from around the world
- Native population – significant

Differences
- Size – Alaska large, Hawai'i small
- Climate – Alaska with long, cold winters, Hawai'i tropical and warm
- Natural resources – Alaska many, Hawai'i few
- Immigrant population – Alaska mainly from within the United States, Hawai'i from all over the world

- Each pattern incorporates transitional words and phrases to compare and contrast ideas.

- Each paragraph uses specific examples and vivid descriptions to emphasize the similarities and differences between the subjects.

- Note how the similar-dissimilar example emphasizes the differences between Alaska and Hawai'i.

Practical Suggestions

- One way to develop a subject for a comparison and contrast paragraph is to divide a sheet of paper into two columns and then list the similarities in one column and the dissimilarities in another. The lists will provide a starting point and allow you to analyze which specific pattern best suits your needs.

- The alternating and block patterns offer fairly objective views of the subjects, and are useful when the writer wants simply to put information in front of the reader for analysis. In contrast, the similar-dissimilar pattern allows the writer to emphasize the similarities or differences; it is therefore more effective for persuasive writing.

- A comparison and contrast paragraph can involve several subjects. For example, you can use a comparison and contrast paragraph to discuss the past, present, and future of a particular subject. (See *Writing a Chronological Paragraph*). You can also use comparison and contrast to discuss three related but different subjects. For example, a similar-dissimilar pattern would be effective in discussing soccer, football, and rugby, three sports that grew from common roots.

WRITING A CLIMACTIC PARAGRAPH

The climactic method of organization is often visualized as a pyramid or a stairway. It begins with a discussion of the least important aspect of a subject—the base of the pyramid or the bottom of the stairs—and moves step by step to the most important aspect of the subject—the top of the pyramid or stairs. The writer must provide a clear path from the least important point to the most important point to ensure that the most important point is not "lost" in the middle of the paragraph.

Using appropriate transitions is vital to guiding the reader along the path. Key transitional words and phrases (e.g., initially, even more important, of greater consequence, most significant of all) act as logical connectors to lead the reader from one point to the next.

Besides using transitions to show the development of ideas from the least to the most important, writers sometimes devote more space (such as including additional supporting details) to each successive idea. By committing more space, the writer provides more weight to the more important opinions or arguments.

To create a climactic paragraph, list the points you wish to make on a piece of paper and number them from least to most important. Then, write the paragraph using the order you have just established, using transitional words and phrases to guide the way.

Several types of writers use the climactic method. Fiction writers use it to intensify the conflict between protagonists and antagonists, until the story reaches a climax where the protagonist makes a key decision or takes a key action. Persuasive writers, such as editorialists and essayists, use the climactic method to provide power to their arguments. These writers begin with small points that the reader will almost certainly agree with, and lead the reader to the most important point, hoping that the reader will be convinced by the series of increasingly important points.

Example

Manufacturing companies implement safety plans for their employees for a variety of reasons. At its most basic level, a safety plan makes good economic sense. When employees miss work due to injury, plant productivity and profits fall. An even more important economic consideration is worker compensation insurance premiums. When too many workers are injured on the job, increases in premiums can be substantial. The only way a company can avoid paying higher premiums is to make sure injuries do not happen in the first place. The most significant reason for a safety plan, though, is not purely economic. Most companies care about their employees and take every step possible to prevent employee injury or death. Even if the safety plan requires expensive steps, most companies will place a greater value on human life than pure profits.

Analysis

- The topic sentence not only states the main idea, but it also tells the reader that the rest of the paragraph will include several reasons to back up the main idea. This is called an organizational clue.

- The subsequent sentences present the supporting ideas, beginning with the least important and ending with the most important.

- Transitional expressions (at its most basic level, an even more important consideration, the most significant reason) both link and separate the supporting points to create climactic paragraph development and to emphasize the increasing importance of each point. (See *Coherence*).

- Compare the structure of this paragraph with the anticlimactic paragraph. (See *Writing an Anticlimactic Paragraph*).

Practical Suggestions

- Use the climactic method to write about events and experiences in your life, particularly when you want to build toward an exciting or interesting climax.

- The climactic method is also excellent for argumentative pieces such as letters to the editor, letters of complaint, or essays designed to change people's points of view or encourage political action.

- Many speechwriters use the climactic method to build toward a stirring climax.

- Combine the climactic and enumerative methods. (See *Writing an Enumerative Paragraph*). It is natural to use the climactic and enumerative methods together to produce clearly organized information and arguments that end with the most important points. (See *Combining Paragraph Structures*).

WRITING AN ANTICLIMACTIC PARAGRAPH

The anticlimactic method of organizing ideas can be visualized as an inverted pyramid or a set of stairs leading downward. In the anticlimactic paragraph, the most important ideas are presented first, followed by ideas of lesser importance, and ending with the least important idea. This is exactly the opposite of the climactic method, in which the most important ideas are presented last. (See *Writing a Climactic Paragraph*).

To write an anticlimactic paragraph, first make a list of all of the points you wish to make. Next, number the list from most important to least important. Then, write your paragraph using the order you just established. Use transitional words and phrases to help your reader understand that the most important idea is first, followed by ideas of lesser importance.

The anticlimactic method of organizing is an effective way to present objective, factual information. Newspaper and magazine reporters frequently use this method because they wish to present factual information in an organized fashion and because many newspaper and magazine readers do not finish the entire story. With the important information up front, the writer ensures that the reader will read at least the main ideas.

Example

Manufacturing companies implement safety plans for their employees for a variety of reasons. The most significant reason for a safety plan is not, as one might think, purely economic. Most companies care about their employees and take every step possible to prevent employee injury or death. Even if the safety plan requires expensive steps, most companies will place a greater value on human life than pure profits. Of course, economic considerations also support good safety plans. Perhaps the key economic consideration is the high worker compensation insurance premiums that must be paid when too many workers are injured on the job. Increases in premiums for companies can be substantial, and the only way for a company to avoid these higher premiums is to make sure the injuries do not happen in the first place. Finally, when employees miss work due to injury, plant productivity and profits fall, which is one more reason companies implement safety plans.

Analysis

- The topic sentence not only states the main idea, but it also tells the reader that the rest of the paragraph will include several reasons to back up the main idea. This is called an organizational clue.

- The subsequent sentences present the supporting ideas, beginning with the most important and ending with the least important.

- Transitional expressions (the most significant, reason, perhaps the key economic reason, of course, finally) both link and separate the supporting points to create anticlimactic paragraph development. (See *Coherence*).

- Compare the structure of this paragraph with the climactic paragraph. (See *Writing a Climactic Paragraph*).

Practical Suggestions

- Use the anticlimactic method to stress the most important idea to your reader first. This is particularly important if you are concerned that the reader might not read the entire piece. For example, a company recruiter or university admissions officer may read hundreds of application letters. It is unlikely the officer will read every cover letter in its entirety, so it is important for an applicant to put the most important information first.

- The anticlimactic method is also effective for letters to the editor or when speaking at public hearings. Most newspapers edit letters for length, and often the cuts come from the end of letters. If the letter is written using the anticlimactic method, only secondary points will get cut and the most important points will remain. At public hearings, it is common for speakers to get cut off after a short time, so anticlimactic organization will make sure the important points are heard.

- Writers also use the anticlimactic method when they write about a subject that they know only appeals to some people. Casual readers can read the first lines, get the general point, and stop reading. Truly interested readers will continue to read to get a full understanding of the secondary points.

WRITING
A GENERAL
TO PARTICULAR
PARAGRAPH

The general to particular method of organizing ideas, also known as deduction, is the most common way to write logical paragraphs. The vast majority of all explanatory and argumentative writing falls into this pattern.

The key to writing a deductive paragraph is to put the most important idea first, in the topic sentence. The idea should be broad enough to need further development, but specific enough to write about in a single paragraph. (See *Topic Sentence*).

Next, the writer follows the generalization with specific facts, examples, observations, experiences, comparisons, descriptions, and other forms of detailed information that help explain the general statement. As the reader moves through the paragraph, the subject, idea, or position set forth in the topic sentence becomes increasingly understandable.

Visually, the deductive arrangement of ideas looks like an inverted pyramid (▼) or a backwards "7." As readers move through the paragraph, the main idea (topic sentence) is developed through more detailed supporting sentences.

```
_____  Topic Sentence
_____
_____
_____
_____          Supporting  Sentences
_____
_____
_____
```

The general to particular structure forms the "backbone" of much of the writing we see every day. Newspaper reporters use it to describe their subjects; editorial writers use it to argue their points; and students use it to answer their exam questions. A careful review of this book would reveal that the most common paragraph type is the general to particular paragraph.

Example

People contemplating a move to Hawai'i should be aware of the high costs of living in an "island paradise." The high costs of food, transportation, and housing may affect a newcomer's lifestyle and economic future. For example, food of all types costs significantly more in Hawai'i than on the Mainland. Newcomers are not particularly surprised that foods shipped to Hawai'i are more expensive than on the Mainland. What is surprising to them, however, is that foods grown in Hawai'i, such as sugar or Kona coffee, are also more expensive than on the Mainland! In addition to food, automobile and gasoline prices both reflect the high cost of shipping to Hawai'i, with gasoline prices as much as sixty cents per gallon more than in the rest of the country. Most of all, however, the prices of homes and land have soared beyond the reach of newcomers. It is not unusual for a small three-bedroom home, located away from the ocean and on a small piece of land, to cost more than $350,000. These prices have not only discouraged some who would like to move to Hawai'i, but they have even forced Hawai'i residents to move away to find more affordable places on the Mainland. The high cost of living is a factor that anyone thinking of moving to Hawai'i must consider.

Analysis

- The writer begins with the main idea—newcomers should be aware of the high cost of living in Hawai'i. (See *Topic Sentence*).

- The writer then develops the main idea through three specific examples: food, transportation, and housing. (See *Writing a Paragraph Using Division* and *Writing an Example Paragraph*).

- Note how the writer uses transitional words and phrases (in addition, most of all) to connect the examples with each other and with the topic sentence. The writer organizes the examples with the most important one at the end to emphasize the point of the paragraph. (See *Writing a Climactic Paragraph*).

Practical Suggestions

- Make sure you pick a subject that is appropriate for development in one paragraph. If it is too broad, consider breaking it into two or more paragraphs. (See *Length and Development*).

- Make sure that all details supporting the topic sentence are accurate, relevant, and representative. (See *Unity*).

- Make sure you provide enough supporting information to back up your main idea and sufficient detail to explain your supporting points.

- Review your paragraph to ensure you did not leave out a step in the explanation. This will help you avoid "jumping to conclusions."

- Compare this structure with the particular to general format, which leads the reader from particular examples to the main idea at the end of the paragraph. (See *Writing a Particular to General Paragraph*).

WRITING A PARTICULAR TO GENERAL PARAGRAPH

The particular to general method of organizing ideas, also know as induction, is a less common form of writing logical paragraphs. Only a fraction of expository and argumentative writing falls into this pattern. But this does not mean that this method is ineffective.

The key to writing an inductive paragraph is to begin with a sentence that introduces the subject, yet does not provide the main idea of the paragraph. In other words, the writer begins by telling the reader what the subject is, but not telling the reader what the writer has to say about that subject. Next, the writer provides support in the form of specific facts, examples, observations, experiences, comparisons, descriptions, and other forms of detailed information.

Once all of the specifics have been presented, the writer provides a general statement, or main idea, as a final topic sentence. If done correctly, the initial specifics and supporting sentences will lead the reader directly to the conclusion presented in the topic sentence. The topic sentence will feel like a natural "summing up" of what the specific sentences have stated.

The idea of moving from particular to general comes from the experiments and ideas of Sir Francis Bacon. Called induction, from the Latin word *inducere*, it means "to lead." This pattern does just that. It leads the reader from one specific point to the next, with the conclusion following logically and naturally from the specific points.

Visually, the inductive arrangement of ideas looks like a pyramid (▲) or an "L." As readers move through the specific examples (supporting sentences), the main idea and purpose (topic sentence) become clear.

Supporting Sentences

Topic Sentence

Example

There are a number of factors that influence a decision whether to move to Hawai'i. For example, food of all types costs significantly more in Hawai'i than on the Mainland. Newcomers are not particularly surprised that foods shipped to Hawai'i are more expensive than on the Mainland. What is surprising to them, however, is that foods grown in Hawai'i, such as sugar or Kona coffee, are also more expensive than on the Mainland! In addition to food, automobile and gasoline prices both reflect the high cost of shipping to Hawai'i, with gasoline prices as much as sixty cents per gallon more than in the rest of the country. Most of all, however, the prices of homes and land have soared beyond the reach of newcomers. It is not unusual for a small three-bedroom home, located away from the ocean and on a small piece of land, to cost more than $350,000. These prices have not only discouraged some who would like to move to Hawai'i, but they have even forced Hawai'i residents to move away to find more affordable places on the Mainland. Therefore, people contemplating a move to Hawai'i should be aware that the costs of living in an "island paradise," as exemplified by the high food, transportation, and housing prices, may affect their lifestyle and economic future.

Analysis

- The writer introduces the subject and then immediately shifts to a series of specific examples. These examples lead the reader to the topic sentence: that people contemplating a move to Hawai'i must consider the high cost of living.

- The paragraph reverses the division pattern of organization by summing up the parts of the whole at the end of the paragraph only after having first discussed the individual parts. (See *Writing a Paragraph Using Division*).

Practical Suggestions

- Ensure that the conclusion follows logically from the information that precedes it. If not, your writing will be considered *non sequitur*, which means that the conclusion does not follow logically from the premise.

- Include enough supporting information and details about your main idea to make your views convincing. Do not leave out important details, or you will be "jumping to conclusions" when you present the topic sentence.

- A particular to general paragraph can be an effective way to introduce a topic. Specific examples grab the reader's attention and lead to the topic sentence, which can then be explored and explained more fully in succeeding paragraphs. (See *Writing an Introductory Paragraph*).

- Unlike the general to particular form for writing paragraphs, the particular to general form requires that the reader finish the paragraph in order to gain a complete understanding of the writer's point of view. This is because the topic sentence is placed at the end.

WRITING A SIMPLE TO COMPLEX PARAGRAPH

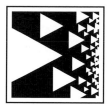

Writers use simple to complex paragraphs to lead the reader step by step from ideas that are easy to grasp to ones that are more difficult to understand. This paragraph style, also known as the building block approach, can be applied to both real and abstract processes. For example, a math teacher may discuss simple algebraic formulas before moving on to complicated calculus formulas. Likewise a student might define freedom in practical terms such as traveling and voting before discussing freedom in philosophical terms.

The important element in writing a simple to complex paragraph is to know your audience. Evaluate the depth of the reader's knowledge before you begin. You do not want to insult a sophisticated audience by oversimplifying a subject, nor do you want to confuse a beginning audience by writing at too complex a level.

The simple to complex paragraph is appropriate for subjects that are difficult to explain. Your goal is to use simple concepts to explain a complex one. It is often easiest to develop this type of paragraph in reverse order.

Start with your complex final subject, and then work backwards using similar but simpler subjects as examples, analogies, or explanations. When the reader approaches the paragraph from the beginning, the simpler examples, analogies, or explanations will act as building blocks to help the reader understand the complex final subject.

Example

One of the most fascinating aspects of life is how some people make difficult tasks look easy. For example, pairs figure skaters glide around the ice with apparent ease. It is only when we look closely that we recognize that the pair is skating backwards, at full speed, in time with music, and while holding hands. Similarly, when we see a professional baseball team turn a "routine" double play, we remark, "It looks so easy." Behind the scenes, however, are years of training and practice. The difficulty of a double play is made apparent simply by witnessing a little league team attempt the same feat. When performed by children, there is no such thing as a "routine" double play; they are all difficult. The same is true of a good marriage. We see an elegant, middle-aged couple, communicating with each other as if by telepathy, and think that married life will be a state of everlasting bliss and happiness. In truth, however, successful marriages are difficult to achieve; they require constant work, communication, and compromise. The couples who make it look so easy are usually the ones who are working the hardest.

Analysis

- This paragraph provides examples on three levels of complexity. The paragraph moves from the seemingly simple feat of ice skaters performing a routine together, to the more intricate teamwork of baseball infielders turning a double play, to the difficult and complex interaction of a husband and wife who have developed their relationship through years of hard work.

- This would be a good paragraph to use with a young audience who is familiar with sports but unfamiliar with love and relationships. The use of sports analogies would help the audience understand that just because a relationship looks easy, it requires at least as much practice and attention as does a difficult sporting feat.

- The writer combines the simple to complex and the particular to general methods of arranging ideas. Note how the main idea appears at the end of the paragraph. (See *Writing a Particular to General Paragraph*).

Practical Suggestions

- Choose the simple to complex method of organizing when you need to move step by step to explain a complex subject.

- This method is an effective way to organize a textbook or a descriptive essay. The writer can build upon what has come before to discuss more difficult topics.

- Know your audience. Most subjects can be both easy and difficult to understand, depending on the reader's prior knowledge and experience. For example, a computer programmer will quickly grasp a paragraph about software applications, but an eighth grader will not. Similarly, attorneys will understand a new copyright law better than will lay people, because attorneys have a better frame of reference from which to analyze the new law. Thus, adjust the level of simplicity with which you begin your paragraph according to your audience.

- The simple to complex method of organizing ideas can be used as the basis for writing longer pieces such as a reports, chapters, or books.

WRITING
AN OPINION AND REASON
PARAGRAPH

Using opinion and reason is a fairly natural process. When speaking, we often say, "I like this one the best because..." or "I think you are the right person for the job because...." Verbal statements such as these are spontaneous, natural, and often filled with emotion. Writing paragraphs using opinion and reason can also be quite natural, but perhaps not as spontaneous. When we write, we have more time to reflect and organize our thoughts. Consequently, written opinions and reasons should be more rational, systematic, and logical than spoken ones.

To write an opinion and reason paragraph, first state an opinion. Then support it with relevant ideas and examples. The opinion should be broad enough to require support, but narrow enough so the support can be provided in a single paragraph. The reasons supporting the opinion should be logical, objective, and based on facts, evidence, observation, or experience.

Three common errors frequently found in opinion and reason paragraphs include: (1) flawed reasoning; (2) insufficient supporting reasons; and (3) insufficiently developed reasons. To avoid these mistakes, examine your written reasons to make sure that they actually support your opinion (rather than just restate it), that you have provided all of the major reasons supporting your opinion, and that the reader can understand each reason.

Example

College students learn many abstract concepts during their studies, but often they do not learn how to apply these concepts to a job. To create a better balance between abstract book knowledge and practical work skills, students should enroll in cooperative education programs that offer them real-life job opportunities where they can apply classroom concepts. Several studies have concluded that students who participate in cooperative education programs perform better on the job than their peers who do not participate in such programs. Students with "co-op" experience are more efficient, receive better evaluations, and get more promotions and raises. Clearly, the benefits of cooperative education programs warrant serious attention from college students looking to improve their future job prospects and performance.

Analysis

- This opinion and reason paragraph provides an argument in favor of a college curriculum that adds practical work experience to abstract classroom theory. Specifically, the writer wants to convince the reader that cooperative education programs will benefit college students who want to excel in the workforce.

- The writer organizes the paragraph by introducing a problem (lack of practical job skills), providing an opinion as to how to fix the problem

(cooperative education programs), and then set-
ting forth reasons for the opinion. (See *Writing a
Problem and Solution Paragraph*).

- For a longer paragraph, the writer would simply
  include more reasons or expand on the reasons
  already given. The writer could add historical
  data, anecdotal experiences, or employer reports.

- The writer concludes the paragraph by tying
  together the benefits of cooperative programs
  with the opinion that students should consider
  such programs.

Practical Suggestions

- Avoid opinions that are too broad and therefore
  difficult to support. Narrow the general opinion
  down or divide it into several paragraphs.

- Write objectively. Readers are more likely to respond positively to reasons grounded in logic than
  arguments relying on emotion. For example, to
  support an opinion that new federal laws are
  required to reduce drunk driving deaths among
  teenagers, a writer should include information
  regarding the number of accidents, the number of
  injuries and deaths, and the effectiveness of similar laws in other countries. These arguments
  would be more persuasive to more people than
  would a tirade about the moral evils of drinking.

- Present your reasons in a clear, organized form.
  Use one or more of the patterns outlined elsewhere
  in this book to organize your opinion and reason
  paragraphs. Possible organizational patterns include: chronological, enumerative, climactic,

simple to complex, or problem and solution. (See *Writing a Chronological Paragraph*, *Writing an Enumerative Paragraph*, *Writing a Climactic Paragraph*, *Writing a Simple to Complex Paragraph*, and *Writing a Problem and Solution Paragraph*).

- Aim for the right balance of reasons. One supporting sentence is usually insufficient, but avoid the temptation to "tack on" additional reasons just for volume. Readers are not necessarily convinced by the sheer number of reasons. Instead, provide clear, logical, and accurate details that cover each reason you feel is important.

- The opinion and reason pattern is an effective way to organize a response to a "why" question on an exam. To do so, turn the "why" question into a declarative sentence, state your opinion, and then outline your supporting reasons. Use the rest of your answer to develop each reason with details and examples. For example, assume the teacher asks, "Why is it important to write clear paragraphs?" Your response can begin, "It is important to write clear paragraphs because X, Y, and Z." From here you develop each of your reasons for X, Y, and Z: "First, X .... Second, Y.... Third, Z...." (See *Writing an Enumerative Paragraph*). Your reasons can also be organized in climactic order: "First, X.... Even more important, Y.... Most significant of all, Z...." (See *Writing a Climactic Paragraph*).

- To distinguish an opinion from a factual statement, remember that an opinion is debatable. The statement, "Yellow is a color used to indicate caution" is a factual statement. In contrast, "Yellow is the most disgusting color for cars" is an opinion.

WRITING A QUESTION AND ANSWER PARAGRAPH

The question and answer paragraph is an effective way to capture a reader's attention, curiosity, and interest. The organization of a question and answer paragraph is quite simple: the writer first poses a question or series of questions and then follows with answers.

There are three goals that can be achieved by asking a question or series of questions. First, questions set the stage for the topic sentence. Second, they provide focus for the rest of the paragraph. Third, they control the size and content of the paragraph. Note how the following four questions achieve those goals. "Why have school shootings increased during the past decade? Are they due to an increase in the availability of guns? Are they due to poor parenting? Or are they caused by something else?"

After posing a question or series of questions, the writer then provides clear, convincing, and organized answers. By the end of the paragraph, the reader should understand both the questions asked and the writer's answers to those questions.

When the writer asks two or three questions, the answers must be in the same order as the questions. For example, in answering the four questions presented above, the writer would first verify the increase in school shootings, and then follow up with sentences discussing the availability of guns, the effects of parenting on school shootings, and other possible explanations.

Often, the questions posed by the writer are so interrelated that they cannot be answered with a series of independent answering sentences. In these instances, it is perfectly appropriate to "bundle" the answers, so long as all of the questions ultimately are answered.

Example

Have you ever wondered why people choose to become vegetarians? Are you curious about whether a vegetarian diet can satisfy a person's nutritional needs? Wouldn't it be difficult for a vegetarian to avoid meat in restaurants or at dinner parties? For many, becoming a vegetarian is a simple, satisfying, and healthy choice. Doctors and dietitians recognize that a balanced vegetarian diet can satisfy all of a person's nutritional needs. In fact, evidence suggests that a vegetarian diet can be even healthier than a diet with meat because it reduces cholesterol and triglyceride levels and increases the supply of several key vitamins and minerals. Moreover, being a vegetarian today is easier than ever. Most restaurant menus include vegetarian selections. In restaurants without a vegetarian menu, chefs are often happy to "create something delicious" for their vegetarian diners. Overall, becoming a vegetarian today is a logical choice for many.

Analysis

- The writer begins with a fairly broad question, and then immediately focuses the reader's attention with two more specific questions.

- The writer answers each specific question in the order it was asked.

- By answering the two specific questions, the writer is able to conclude with an answer to the original broad question.

- Note how the writer uses transitional words and phrases to guide the reader through the paragraph (in fact, moreover, overall). (See *Coherence*).

- For a longer piece, the writer could develop each part of the answer by writing individual paragraphs about the nutritional benefits and ease of being a vegetarian in today's society.

Practical Suggestions

- When using the question and answer method of organizing a paragraph, remember to answer the main question. It is easy to get caught up in the supporting questions and leave the reader wondering about the main question.

- Make sure your answering sentences are clear, fully developed, and logically organized. Your answer should leave the reader without any unaddressed questions.

- Subjects describing a process are often good candidates for question and answer paragraphs. For example, "How do you repair a leaky faucet?" (See *Writing a Process Analysis Paragraph*).

- Another type of paragraph that works well with question and answer organization is the opinion and reason paragraph. For example, "Is there discrimination in the workplace?" (See *Writing an Opinion and Reason Paragraph*).

WRITING
A PROBLEM AND SOLUTION
PARAGRAPH

The problem and solution method of arranging ideas is an effective way to convey information designed to prompt action. It can be applied to almost every aspect of life, including education, government and politics, family relationships, religion, the arts, or sports.

Writing a problem and solution paragraph is relatively straightforward. The writer begins by stating a problem. Next, the writer sets forth a solution. The remainder of the paragraph is used to develop the solution and explain why it solves the problem presented. The writer can also use the development section of the paragraph to explain why the proposed solution is the best of several alternatives, or why the proposed solution will not cause additional problems.

Problem and solution paragraphs work best when they are well supported and analytical. Readers respond well to a writer who has done the appropriate homework and who explains the problem and solution in clear, logical steps. This often requires substantial research, careful thought, and planning by the writer.

Scientific writers and editorialists are two of the many groups who use problem and solution paragraphs. In scientific writing, the writer presents a scientific question followed by a logical solution. In editorial writing, the writer will raise a social concern and then advocate a position to address that concern.

Example

When considering possible dangers associated with the outdoors, campers and hikers usually think about bears, snakes, floods, fires, and other natural hazards. But there is an even greater hazard to campers and hikers: the "human beast." Recent murders in our state and national parks highlight the difficult problem of preventing crime in our wilderness areas. There are several steps that government and individuals can take to reduce crime. The government can help by increasing police training and improving facility design. A great number of crimes occur in parking lots, and making these areas more open and secure could help a great deal. Individuals can take self-defense training and possibly defeat their attacker. The most important way to make outdoor experiences safer, though, is quite simple: people must use common sense. Campers and hikers must recognize that they do not leave danger behind when they leave the city and must keep a vigilant eye out for signs of danger.

Analysis

- The paragraph uses common outdoor dangers to introduce its real topic, the problem of human crime in our parks and wilderness areas.

- The writer suggests three solutions to the problem, ending with the most important. This is an example of climactic organization. (See *Writing a Climactic Paragraph*).

- The purpose of the paragraph is both to provide information and to stir people into action about retaining a sense of awareness and common sense when traveling to the wild.

Practical Suggestions

- State the problem clearly. The reader must understand exactly what the problem is in order to evaluate the proposed solution.

- State the solution clearly. Do not be vague or rely on guesswork in proposing solutions. If it is necessary to gather data or perform other research to strengthen your solutions, do so. It is difficult to convince your reader of the solution if the reader can tell you have not done your homework.

- The climactic approach, used in the example above, and the question and answer approach are both good methods of arranging ideas for problem and solution paragraphs. (See *Writing a Climactic Paragraph* and *Writing a Question and Answer Paragraph*).

- Sometimes a proposed solution will pose new, unexpected problems that will also need to be addressed. Be aware that complex problems may require more time and critical thinking. It is often easier to state a problem than it is to provide a solution. If there are new questions that cannot be fully answered, admit it. Readers are highly critical when they see a writer ignore obvious problems.

WRITING
A CAUSE AND EFFECT
PARAGRAPH

Cause and effect paragraphs aim at examining outcomes and reasons for outcomes. Put another way, cause and effect paragraphs examine what happened and why it happened. Writers use the cause and effect method of organizing ideas when writing about issues, problems, and solutions. (See *Writing a Problem and Solution Paragraph*).

The words cause and effect define each other. A cause is something that produces an effect; an effect is something brought about by a cause. For example, a heavy rain (cause) can lead to a landslide (effect). Sometimes, an initial cause can lead to an initial effect, but that initial effect can be the cause of a later effect. This can be illustrated by extending the example of heavy rain causing a landslide. The landslide, which was the effect of the heavy rain, can in turn be the cause of a house collapsing into a ravine. In turn, the house collapsing into the ravine can be the cause of someone being hurt. This chain of cause and effect may seem repetitive, but it is quite natural.

The first step in writing a cause and effect paragraph is deciding what the primary organization will be. A cause and effect paragraph can be arranged either by discussing the cause first or by discussing the effect first. In either case, the writer should focus on the relationship between what happens and why it happens.

Within the primary organization, the writer next chooses the internal organization. A cause and effect paragraph can be arranged using the general to particular, particular to general, climactic, or anticlimactic patterns. (See *Writing a General to Particular Paragraph*, *Writing a Particular to General Paragraph*, *Writing a Climactic Paragraph*, and *Writing an Anticlimactic Paragraph*). The choice is whether to put the important information first or to build up to the important information.

Example: Cause to Effect

The media is a powerful force that shapes teenage attitudes towards violence. The print media, meaning magazines and newspapers, routinely carries graphic stories and photographs of violent acts. Teenagers see headlines blaring news of the latest murder or riot. Television and movies do the same, producing show after show in which the hero or heroine is glorified for killing "bad guys" by the dozens. Finally, the internet and video games provide teens with newer and more interactive ways not only to watch violence, but also seemingly to participate in and practice it. It is no wonder that today's teenagers seem much more accepting of violence than were teens of earlier generations.

Example: Effect to Cause

Teenage attitudes towards violence have changed dramatically from attitudes held by previous generations. Teens today seem much more accepting of violence in their world. One of the major causes behind this shift is the media. The print media, meaning newspapers and magazines, routinely carries graphic stories and photographs of violent acts. Teenagers see headlines blaring news of the latest murder or riot. Television and movies do the same, producing show after show in which the hero or heroine is glorified for killing "bad guys" by the dozens. Finally, the internet and video games provide teens with newer and more interactive ways not only to watch violence, but also seemingly to participate in and practice it.

Analysis

- The first example shows how four specific causes from the media—printed material, television, movies, and interactive internet and video games—result in changed teenage attitudes towards violence. The writer uses the general to particular method of organizing when discussing the causes of teen attitudes, first by introducing the media in general, and then by discussing various types of media influences. (See *Writing a General to Particular Paragraph*).

- The second example states the effect first (changed attitudes towards violence) and follows with four specific causes. Again the writer uses the general to particular method of organization.

- In both examples, the media examples are organized in a climactic fashion. The writer begins

135

with print media, which simply shows pictures or prints stories. Next, the writer discusses movies, which show exactly how the violence occurs. Finally, the writer discusses how video and internet games allow readers and viewers to actually participate in the (simulated) violence. (See *Writing a Climactic Paragraph*).

- For longer pieces of writing, each media example could be developed into its own paragraph, with the writer providing additional examples, titles, and internet sites.

Practical Suggestions

- Before you begin writing, carefully distinguish between the causes and the effects. List them on paper. If necessary, make a separate list for each. (See *Planning and Organizing*).

- Beware of false causes and effects. There is a difference between a correlation between two subjects and a true cause and effect relationship. For example, if two redheaded boys won two different running races, a writer might conclude that red hair is the cause of winning races. This would be a false cause and effect. The boys won (effect) because they were fast (cause), not because they had red hair.

- Use examples for support, either for causes or effects. Ensure that your supporting examples are accurate, representative, and convincing.

- Present causes and effects in whatever method is most effective. Possible alternatives include chronological order, climactic, or anticlimactic. (See

Writing a Chronological Paragraph, Writing a Climactic Paragraph, and *Writing an Anticlimactic Paragraph*).

- Use the cause and effect method of arranging ideas to write editorials, argue for social or political change, or take a position on local, national, or international issues.

WRITING A PARAGRAPH USING DIALOGUE

Dialogue is conversation in writing. The conversation can be between two people or among a large group of people. Writers often use dialogue as a way to introduce or conclude a piece of writing, but it can be just as effective within the body of a paragraph or composition. Wherever it is placed, dialogue can be used to tell a story, create interest, add effect, illustrate a point, or vary an explanation or argument.

There are several things to keep in mind when you write dialogue. First, when you are writing a dialogue that includes several persons, you must create a new paragraph every time there is a new speaker. Thus, a paragraph using dialogue can vary from a few words to several sentences long. Second, as you write dialogue, be careful not to overuse the word "said." There are literally hundreds of synonyms for "said," and it is almost certain that one of those synonyms will add more color and style to your writing. Finally, consider varying your dialogue by using a "split" quotation. For example, "Please pass the sugar," asked Sue, "so I can finish making the cookies." Remember that the second segment of a split quotation begins with a lower case letter (unless it is a proper noun or the first word of a new sentence).

Example

"I can't believe the manager is leaving that pitcher in," grumbled Michael. "Can't he see that the pitcher is exhausted? Our whole season is on the line here."

"Yeah," agreed Peggy, "but our bullpen is weak; he's just hoping the starter can make it through this inning." Just as Peggy finished her sentence, there was a loud "crack!" as the batter hit the ball deep into left field. Michael and Peggy turned their heads as the ball soared up into the night and started to descend right at the fence.

"Get it! Get it! Get it!" shouted Michael as the left fielder turned and ran towards the fence.

Peggy chimed in with a few words of her own. "Jump! Jump! You can get it!"

The left fielder jumped, reached back over the fence, caught the ball just as it cleared the top, and brought it back down with him. Peggy turned to Michael with a slight smile, "I knew he could do it. Now we're out of the inning. Maybe the manager knew what he was doing after all."

Analysis

- Rather than describe or tell the story from the first person point of view, the writer uses characters and dialogue to tell the story from the dramatic point of view. (See *Writing a Narrative Paragraph*). The characters bring the reader into the action and create drama and excitement.

- This dialogue could act as an introduction to a composition about the excitement of watching baseball together.

- The writer injects a variety of substitutes for "said" to add greater specificity and variety (grumbled, agreed, shouted, chimed). In the last sentence, the writer does not use said or a synonym for said, because it is clear who is speaking and why.

- The writer puts the quoted words in a variety of places: at the beginning of the sentence, at the end, and split with the "said" words in the middle.

- The story covers only an instant in time. Other dialogues can cover large time periods, with most of the space filled by narration and description and only a few lines of dialogue inserted for effect.

Practical Suggestions

- Place punctuation marks (periods, commas, question marks, exclamation points) inside the quotation marks.

- Use quotation marks for both sides of a split quotation. For example, "Get going," he demanded, "or I'll call the police." This rule applies even if the second part of the split quotation is a complete sentence. In such instances, begin both parts of the split quotation with a capital letter: "Get going," he demanded. "If you don't leave now, I'll call the police."

- Whenever a speaker's words extend for more than one paragraph, use quotation marks at the beginning of the dialogue, at the beginning (but not the end) of every new paragraph of continuing dialogue, and at the very end of the dialogue in the final paragraph.

- Thoughts are never placed in quotations marks. For example: (1) I wondered, why is it that people are living longer today? (2) The music is very soothing, I thought.

- When writers remove themselves from the story and give characters the power to tell the story via dialogue, the story becomes more alive and realistic.

- Dialogue is useful to break up a story. Changing from the third person omniscient point of view (where the narrator describes everyone's thoughts) to using dialogue increases interest, creates liveliness, and adds variety to a writer's style. (See *Writing a Narrative Paragraph*). For example, instead of writing a paragraph describing the fear faced by two soldiers in a battlefield, let the soldiers tell the story by creating a dialogue that explains their fears.

- To add greater specificity and variety to your dialogue, refer to the list of 500 "Substitutes for Said" found in *A Writer's Guide to Transitional Words and Expressions*.

WRITING A NARRATIVE PARAGRAPH

A narrative paragraph tells a story. Generally, a narrative paragraph is written in chronological sequence and often contains dialogue. Because it tells a story, a narrative paragraph must have a storyteller. Therefore, the key decision in writing a narrative paragraph is determining who that narrator will be. In other words, you need to answer the question, "Through whose eyes will the story be told?" A writer can choose to narrate a story from four commonly used points of view: (1) first person point of view; (2) third person omniscient point of view; (3) third person limited point of view; and (4) dramatic point of view.

The first person point of view is also called the subjective point of view because the story is told from the narrator's perspective and includes the narrator's subjective thoughts and impressions. The narrator uses the first person personal pronoun "I" (e.g., "I saw..."; "I heard..."; "I thought..."). Writers who use this point of view frequently write about personal experiences and observations. When fiction writers use the first person point of view, the narrator is either a character in the story itself or an "insider" who observes and comments about others.

In all of the third person points of view, the narrator is not a character in the story, but instead stands outside the story's action. The narrator tells the story using the third person pronouns "he," "she," "it," and "they." Because the third person narrator is not part of the action and tells the story only as an outside observer, these points of view are referred to as "objective" points of view. The third person points of view differ only in the number of characters whose thoughts are known to the narrator.

Omniscient means "all knowing" and the narrator in a story told from the third person omniscient point of view can see all, hear all, know all, and tell all about every character's thoughts, speech, and actions in any place at any time. This point of view allows the writer a great deal of flexibility, but revealing the thoughts of too many characters can lead to confusion. To avoid this problem, authors using the third person omniscient point of view generally reveal the thoughts of only a few major characters.

In the third person limited point of view, the narrator knows the thoughts and actions of only one character, usually the main character in the story. The narrator in this point of view "stands by the elbow" of the main character and tells what happens to the main character (including thoughts and feelings). Because the narrator is "standing by the elbow" of the main character, the narrator only can reveal what the main character sees or senses. This point of view is effective for fiction and particularly suspense novels, because the reader learns of the narrator's thoughts and fears but is left with the same sense of suspense as the narrator.

The final point of view is called the dramatic point of view. In this point of view, the story is told with only objective information—what people say and do, not what they think. Think of the dramatic point of view as a police report, giving just the facts of what occurs. Writers using this point of view cannot convey any character's thoughts or emotions, and instead rely on detailed, vivid factual descriptions to convey this information. For example, rather than saying a character felt angry, the narrator would say the character's face grew red and he began to shout. The narrator might also use dialogue to convey the same idea: Matthew shouted at the top of his lungs, "It's your fault and you're gonna pay!"

The following examples tell the same simple story from each of the different points of view. In each example, notice who is telling the story and whose thoughts are known to the storyteller.

Example: First Person

Narrator is participant; provides only narrator's thoughts and observations.

Kirsten and I were walking down the street. I asked Kirsten, "What do you think of the new boy in school?" I tried to sound casual, but inside I was nervous because I liked the new boy and I was hoping that Kirsten was not interested in him.

"Oh, he's nice," replied Kirsten while she looked away. "He seems pretty funny, too."

Inside, I was seething. Kirsten sounded casual, but I could tell by the way she was avoiding my eyes that she was hiding something.

Example: Third Person Omniscient

Outside narrator knows all and sees all, but usually reveals the thoughts only of the main characters.

Kirsten and Mia were walking down the street. Mia asked Kirsten, "What do you think of the new boy in school?" Mia tried to sound casual, but inside she was nervous because she liked the new boy and was hoping that Kirsten was not interested in him.

"Oh, he's nice," replied Kirsten. "He seems pretty funny, too." Kirsten hoped that she was sounding casual. She could tell Mia was interested in the new boy, and didn't want to let on that she already had a date with him.

Inside, Mia was seething. Although the words sounded casual, Mia could tell by the way Kirsten was avoiding her eyes that Kirsten was hiding something.

Example: Third Person Limited

Outside narrator knows only one character's thoughts.

Kirsten and Mia were walking down the street. Mia asked Kirsten, "What do you think of the new boy in school?" Mia tried to sound casual, but inside she was nervous because she liked the new boy and was hoping that Kirsten was not interested in him.

"Oh, he's nice," replied Kirsten. "He seems pretty funny, too."

Inside, Mia was seething. Although the words sounded casual, Mia could tell by the way Kirsten was avoiding her eyes that Kirsten was hiding something.

Example: Dramatic

Outside narrator provides no thoughts; the entire story is told through words and actions.

Kirsten and Mia were walking down the street. Mia asked Kirsten, "What do you think of the new boy in school?" Mia's face was slightly flushed and she stuttered a bit as she asked this question.

"Oh, he's nice," replied Kirsten in a flat tone while looking away. "He seems pretty funny, too."

Mia walked silently beside Kirsten and did not say anything for quite some time.

Analysis

- Note how changing the point of view can change how the reader views this very simple story. In the first person point of view, the reader identifies with the narrator and experiences her feelings directly. In contrast, the dramatic point of view provides no thoughts, so the reader cannot identify with one character more than the other.

- A change in point of view also alters the need for descriptive words. When the narrator can describe someone's thoughts, there is no need to also describe the facial expressions and other outward indications of those thoughts. In the third person omniscient example, the writer simply tells the characters' thoughts and does not need to describe facial expressions. In the dramatic example, however, the writer must rely entirely on description and actions to tell the story. Note how the dramatic example above has many more adjectives (descriptive words) than the other paragraphs.

- While the dramatic point of view can be limiting, it can also create excitement. In the example above, the reader knows something is going on between Mia and Kirsten, but is not quite sure what. The story has much more suspense and drama than the other points of view. Thus, the name "dramatic" point of view describes it well.

Practical Suggestions

- Once you select a point of view, follow it consistently from beginning to end. In other words, if you begin telling your story from the "I" point of view, do not switch in the middle of a paragraph to telling it from the "he/she/it" point of view.

- Use transitional words and expressions to indicate time order (lately, recently, today, soon after), to show how or when something occurs in time (suddenly, as soon as, all of the time, never), or to indicate sequence (initially, subsequently, later on, in the end). (See *Coherence*).

- Occasionally, it is appropriate to develop a narrative paragraph using the climactic method, leading the reader from the least important event to the most important event. (See *Writing a Climactic Paragraph*).

- In longer compositions, telling a story can be a good technique as an introduction or example.

- Personification is related to the concept of point of view and is an effective way to inject examples in a story. (See *Writing an Example Paragraph*). Writers use personification to give human qualities to animals or inanimate objects. Children's story writers use personification more frequently than any other group of writers by giving their animal characters the abilities to speak, reason, and express emotions.

WRITING AN ANECDOTAL PARAGRAPH

An anecdote is a brief story. Writers often use anecdotes to provide examples, clarify opinions, or present information. An anecdotal paragraph can be an effective way to introduce a topic, or it can be used to add variety to a long piece of explanatory or argumentative writing.

The tone in an anecdote is frequently, but not necessarily, humorous. This is true even though the writer may be using the anecdote to discuss a serious subject. In fact, writers often use a humorous anecdote as a counterpoint to a serious subject, hiding the serious subject within the humorous story, where it is unknown to the participants in the story but obvious to the reader. For example, in a composition about how teenagers think they are invincible and take foolish risks, the subjects of the anecdote may tell a hilarious story (at least to them) about how they drove drunk last night, but the reader recognizes that although the facts of the story may seem funny, the problem of teenage drinking and driving is very real.

Many anecdotes contain dialogue. Remember that a new paragraph must be created for each new speaker.

Example: Anecdote With Dialogue

We acquire words based on our geographical experience. In Hawai'i, for example, local residents use the word "Mainland" to refer to the contiguous forty-eight states. You would never hear the following conversation in Hawai'i unless it were between two people who did not grow up or move there.

"Did you see the TV weather report last night?" asked John, as he came up out of the surf toward his wife Sheila, who was reading in a lounge chair on the beach.

"No, but I bet it's cold back in the States," Sheila replied, smiling happily that they had decided to spend Christmas break on Maui.

"Cold is not the word," John declared. "It was freezing back in the States."

Hawai'i residents know from their geographical experience that Hawai'i, too, is a state, and are somewhat sensitive to implications that it is not. That is why Hawai'i residents do not use the word "States" unless they mean all fifty states.

Example: Narrative Anecdote

When I first moved to Hawai'i from Chicago, I quickly learned that where you live has an effect on how you use language. One time I used the phrase, "It sure is cold back in the States." I was corrected immediately, and kindly informed that Hawai'i is the 50th state, and that the correct reference to the 48 contiguous states (excluding Hawai'i and Alaska) is the "Mainland." Having never lived on an island, the word Mainland had never become part of my vocabulary. Even though I knew U.S. history,

I led my listener to believe I didn't, and offended him at the same time. Geography, I concluded, certainly does shape language.

Analysis

- Both examples discuss the same idea—that geography influences language usage. Both examples also use the same basic story, that Hawai'i residents have adopted the word "Mainland" to refer to the 48 contiguous states, to illustrate this idea.

- In the first example, the writer states the main idea in a topic sentence and then uses dialogue as an example to help explain the topic sentence. Note how the writer uses a new paragraph for each new speaker. (See *Writing a Paragraph Using Dialogue*).

- The writer adds a humorous touch, which not only keeps the reader's interest, but may also help the reader to remember the point of the story.

- In the second example, the writer uses the first person point of view. This view allows the writer to insert emotions into the story and therefore make it more personal.

- The personal anecdote in the second example includes some of the writer's own words, identified by quotation marks, that add variety to the writing style.

Practical Suggestions

- An anecdote is a useful way to introduce a subject because it captures a reader's interest and provides a "real world" application for your subject.

- Anecdotes are flexible. You can use as much or as little dialogue as you wish and any of the narrative points of view (first person, third person omniscient, third person limited, dramatic). (See *Writing a Paragraph Using Dialogue* and *Writing a Narrative Paragraph*).

- Avoid using more than one anecdote in a short piece of writing.

- Keep anecdotes short and simple.

- Use an anecdotal paragraph to clarify a point, to "break up" a long piece of writing, to add variety to your writing style, and to make your writing more interesting.

WRITING
AN INTRODUCTORY
PARAGRAPH

An introductory paragraph sets the stage for additional paragraphs in a body of writing to follow. An effective introductory paragraph has several purposes. It must draw the reader's interest, define the subject or purpose of the composition, and provide organizational and style clues to help the reader understand the structure of the composition.

Within each introductory paragraph should be one or two sentences containing the main idea of the composition. Called the "thesis statement," this sentence or sentences must be crafted carefully to fulfill several important functions. First, the thesis statement should clearly state the main idea of the composition. In addition, the thesis should state a position rather than merely state a fact. This will provide focus for the composition. Finally, the thesis statement should define the length of the composition; it must be broad enough to warrant more than one paragraph of development, but not too broad for development within the allotted space. The generality or specificity of a thesis statement will vary depending on whether your goal is to create a short composition or write an entire book.

In addition to containing the thesis statement, an introductory paragraph should also provide clues about the style and organization of the rest of the composition. Organizational clues are references to subjects that will be discussed in later paragraphs. Writers often write one sentence in the introductory paragraph for each paragraph to follow. Each such sentence in the introductory paragraph provides a brief summary of the subject that will be discussed fully in its corresponding later paragraph.

One way to think about an introductory paragraph is to compare it with an appetizer. Before we have a main meal, we whet our appetites with food and drink. An introductory paragraph is much the same, except that it focuses on stimulating our thoughts and ideas rather than our appetites.

Example

Books greatly influence people's perceptions and attitudes about women's roles in society. Much of this influence is positive, as books can help people understand the contributions of women to society. Some of this influence, however, is negative, particularly when old, outdated materials linger on the shelves of school and public libraries longer than they should. Two books that should have been removed long ago from school and public libraries exemplify the negative impact books can have. The first book, *Men and Machines*, contains pictures of men in positions of power and innovation and women in positions of subservience and service. The second book, *America's Leadership*, discusses leadership using only the "he" point of view. Each of these books, discussed below, subtly damages egos and lowers self-esteem and should be removed from libraries serving our children.

Analysis

- The paragraph provides the reader with a broad thesis sentence, adds sufficient detail to narrow and focus the thesis, and then provides clues about the rest of the composition.

- The writer stirs interest by presenting both positive and negative statements, and then states a clear opinion about the importance of removing outdated, sexist books from our libraries. The reader may not necessarily agree with this position, as a strong argument can be made that it is unhealthy in a democracy to allow one person to judge what books are good for people and what books are bad for people. Regardless of whether the reader agrees, the thesis is clear and understandable.

- The paragraph concludes with an introduction to two books that will be discussed in greater detail later in the composition. These organizational clues prepare the reader for a detailed discussion of each of the books as supporting examples for the thesis. (See *Writing an Example Paragraph* and *Writing a Paragraph Using Division*).

- The paragraph is a unified whole. All sentences are interrelated and focus on the same subject. (See *Unity*).

Practical Suggestions

- There are several good ways to draw a reader's attention in an introductory paragraph. Some of these ways include quotations, examples, questions, personal experiences, anecdotes, or even absurd statements.

- As you move to your thesis statement, be concrete and use direct declarative statements. Avoid generalizations that include all-inclusive words such as every, all, everyone, anyone, and no one.

- Avoid the word "I" in your thesis statement. Statements such as "I am going to write about..." or "I think..." do not lead to strong declarative thesis statements. Simply drop the "I" phrase and try to restate your thesis in another way.

- Limit the idea or subject of your thesis statement to one point so the task of writing supporting paragraphs does not become monumental.

- Do not confuse a thesis statement with a topic sentence. A thesis statement is the subject of an entire composition, while a topic sentence presents the main point of an individual paragraph. (See *Topic Sentence*).

WRITING
A TRANSITIONAL
PARAGRAPH

Writers use transitional paragraphs to bridge ideas or to shift from one idea to another. Transitional paragraphs help a reader follow the writer's thoughts from one subject to another subject.

There are many ways to organize transitional paragraphs. Among the most common are: (1) summarizing; (2) using the paragraph hook; (3) shifting the point of view; and (4) asking questions.

In the first approach, the writer summarizes the idea set forth in the preceding paragraph and then introduces a new point. This technique is useful when comparing and contrasting two subjects.

The second approach is similar to the first. The writer echoes key phrases or concepts from the earlier paragraph before moving in a different direction or introducing another idea. This repetition "hooks" the reader and brings the reader along to the new point. (See *Coherence*).

The third approach, shifting the point of view, is useful when a writer wishes to shift from an individual to a collective point of view. For example, a transitional paragraph is useful when shifting from using "I" (perhaps describing a personal experience) to using "we" (when referring to a larger group of individuals who have had similar experiences or to people in general). It is also useful to reverse this process, shifting from a broad discussion to a specific example. Finally, writers use this approach to change the tone of a composition, such as from serious to humorous or vice versa.

The fourth approach, in which the writer asks a question or series of questions, is a useful way to move from one subject to another subject with similar issues, or to point out that despite the earlier paragraphs, questions remain that deserve further discussion.

Example

Note: This example shows the end of a previous paragraph, followed by the complete transitional paragraph, and then the beginning of the following paragraph.

...These methods are but a few examples of how we as a society are addressing some of the needs of victims of alcoholism.

While victims of alcoholism have captured national attention and resources, victims of child abuse receive much less attention and little of our public resources. There are relatively few shelters for child abuse victims, and a shocking number of abused children end up homeless on the streets of our larger cities. One possible way we as a society can address the needs of child abuse victims is to encourage counselors and parents to organize support groups like those that have proven so effective in dealing with the effects of alcoholism.

The idea of forming support groups for victims of child abuse is not new in other countries. In Australia, one support group, founded in 1995, is Advocates for Survivors of Child Abuse....

Analysis

- The writer uses the transitional paragraph to shift from the subject of alcoholism treatment to the subject of child abuse treatment. The transitional paragraph provides an opportunity for readers to see the similarities between the two subjects, while keeping the two subjects separate and distinct.

- Note how the writer repeats an important idea (how we as a society respond to a group in need) as a way to bring the reader from one subject to the next.

- In this paragraph, there is no single, distinct, topic sentence. Instead, there are two related topic sentences. The first sentence echoes the ideas of the previous paragraph, and the last sentence leads into the following paragraph.

Practical Suggestions

- A transitional paragraph can be short (as few as two to three sentences) or long. Paragraph length is determined by how complex the subject is as well as by the background or introductory information required to prepare the reader for the subject to follow. (See *Length and Development*).

- Transitional paragraphs are particularly useful for longer pieces of writing such as reports, essays, and book chapters.

- Guard against the temptation to put too much information in your transitional paragraph. The transitional paragraph should serve as a transition between two subjects; it should not attempt to summarize or repeat either subject.

- A transitional paragraph may act as a mini-conclusion for the content that precedes it and a mini-introduction for the content to follow.

- If something less than a full transitional paragraph is needed, refer to *A Writer's Guide to Using Eight Methods of Transition* for additional transitional techniques.

WRITING A CONCLUDING PARAGRAPH

Just as a tasty dessert is the perfect ending to a satisfying meal, an artful concluding paragraph is the perfect ending to a well-crafted composition. A concluding paragraph wraps up all of the loose ends of a composition and answers any lingering questions. Just like a dessert, it leaves the reader with a satisfied, complete feeling.

A concluding paragraph is not necessarily a summary of what came before. (See *Writing a Summary Paragraph*). Instead, a concluding paragraph can be a variety of things. It can be an answer to a question posed in an earlier paragraph; it can be a call to action following a series of paragraphs laying out a problem and possible solutions; or it can be a restatement, in different words, of the main idea of the composition. All of these are legitimate concluding paragraphs and all have certain features in common.

First, a concluding paragraph should have a clearly focused statement that wraps up the piece. Often this statement comes at the end of the paragraph. It can be in a single sentence or perhaps two sentences, but it must "pull everything together" for the reader. After reading this statement, the reader should understand the purpose of the entire piece.

Second, a concluding paragraph should not introduce totally new ideas. The conclusion is meant to finish the written piece, not leave the reader expecting more. Sometimes, however, the goal of a written piece is to point out where questions still remain; the concluding paragraph certainly could end with unanswered questions. For example, after reviewing all of the evidence, a composition about the possibility of extra-terrestrial life could conclude with the ultimate question, "Is there anybody else out there?"

Finally, a concluding paragraph must maintain unity with the rest of the piece. In other words, the concluding paragraph must relate to the ideas introduced earlier.

Example

Note: This example paragraph concludes an article describing various ways a resort area can attract visitors and encourage them to return.

Formal improvements, such as changing the name of the "Tourist Information Center" to "Visitor Information Center," and organizing merchants to offer free or discounted coupons to local attractions are two effective ways to attract visitors and encourage them to return. These improvements by themselves, however, will not do the job. The single most important factor is to convince your local residents to be friendly. Employ friendly, congenial people in visitor-related businesses and do whatever you can to turn everyone in town into a welcome sign with a happy face. Follow these basic rules and visitors will not only keep coming, but they will also bring their families and friends. The result will be a thriving economy for your resort town.

Analysis

- The paragraph contains a single, clearly focused statement wrapping up the point of the composition. The writer believes that friendly people are the key to attracting visitors to a resort area, and the paragraph clearly states this belief.

- The paragraph contains a call to action and hoped-for results from that action. The writer exhorts the reader to combine concrete changes (signage, discounts) with changes in attitude (encouraging friendliness), which hopefully will be a boon for the town's economy.

- The concluding paragraph maintains unity with the rest of the article. One method of maintaining unity is to repeat key phrases. (See *Coherence*). Here, the writer repeats a phrase that could have been in the introductory paragraph: "attract visitors and encourage them to return." This repetition strengthens the unity of the article and tells the reader that the question posed at the beginning is being answered.

Practical Suggestions

- Do not use up all of your good ideas in the introduction or body of a composition. Save at least one good idea or phrase for your concluding paragraph to use as a clinching sentence.

- If you are having trouble finding a strong concluding statement, one idea is to make your concluding statement "echo" the thesis in your introductory paragraph. When you use this technique to conclude, do not state the thesis word for word; instead, rephrase it without altering its meaning or purpose.

- If your paper is short, there is no need to repeat your earlier ideas because your reader will be able to remember what came before. On the other hand, if your paper is long, repeating a key phrase or example may be appropriate.

- If your subject deals with a problem or controversy, end with a possible solution if you can.

- If there is no good answer to the question you are faced with, make it clear in your concluding paragraph that the problem is not yet solved.

- Avoid writing conclusions by saying, "As I have already said...."

- Avoid weak conclusions that you just "tack on" when you run out of ideas. Good conclusions must be thought out carefully.

- Like the conclusion of a good song, make your endings strong. Give the reader a sense of completion and finality.

WRITING A SUMMARY PARAGRAPH

A summary paragraph contains a review of earlier points as a way of tying together an entire composition. Summaries generally are reserved for longer pieces of writing, where it is necessary to first remind the reader of earlier points before tying them together. In shorter pieces, it is not necessary to remind the reader of earlier points, and a concluding paragraph may be more appropriate. (See *Writing a Concluding Paragraph*).

To make the distinction between a concluding paragraph and a summary paragraph clearer, think of a conclusion as a final analysis of your day's activities, such as, "Overall, it has been a good day." In contrast, think of a summary as a final review of what you accomplished during an entire week, such as, "On Monday and Tuesday, work was stressful, and I did not achieve my goals; on Wednesday and Thursday, I completed a long-term project; and on Friday I got more done than on Monday and Tuesday put together. Overall, my work was only semi-productive."

There are several ways to organize a summary paragraph, but one of the most common is a simple, two-step process. First, take the topic sentences from each of the body paragraphs and restate them in the summary paragraph. The restated topic sentences should be in the same order as the paragraphs. Second, take the thesis statement from the introduction and restate it to conclude your piece. This method reminds the reader where he or she has been, and then finishes with a strong restatement of the main idea of the piece.

Example

Note: This example summarizes a long article that focuses on six different approaches to treating cancer.

Thus, there are several important avenues anyone who has been diagnosed with cancer should consider. By far the most important approach is using modern treatments such as radiation, chemotherapy, and other drugs. For many patients, this is the first and final choice. Another choice is traditional Chinese acupuncture. This approach is the least accepted, and its results are often temporary. A regimen of vitamin and mineral supplements may also help, but heavy dosages can create adverse side effects. Natural, fresh herbs and herbal products can be helpful, but patients must be careful to avoid the empty promises of charlatans. Changes in diet are important, but a dietitian should be involved in picking the right combination of foods. Finally, a change in lifestyle is an important choice for each cancer patient. Avoiding stress and keeping a positive mental attitude are vital. Not all of these choices are for everyone, but every cancer patient should explore the range of options available to combat this horrible disease.

Analysis

- The summary first presents a statement based on each topic sentence in the magazine article, and follows with a restatement of the thesis statement of the entire article and a hint of the author's opinion regarding cancer treatment.

- The article and the summary are both written in anticlimactic order. The treatment the author considers most important (modern cancer therapies) is listed first, with less important treatments following. (See *Writing an Anticlimactic Paragraph*). One interesting twist to the order is the insertion of a positive mental attitude as a factor in treatment. Clearly the author believes this is important, but it is not formally a treatment, so the author puts it last. This placement both differentiates and emphasizes attitude from the other treatments.

- The word "thus" signals the beginning of a summary. Other common transitional expressions are "in summary" and "to summarize." (See *Coherence*).

Practical Suggestions

- Summarize the main points in the same order in which they were presented.

- Search out ideas for the summary by reviewing the topic sentences and the thesis statement.

- If you have difficulty writing a summary, write out each topic sentence and your thesis statement word for word in a new paragraph. Then rewrite these sentences to create a summary. The summary may be slightly stilted, but it is a good place to start.

- Avoid using "in conclusion" as a summary transition. By keeping the transitional expressions for summary and conclusion paragraphs separate, you will keep the types of paragraphs separate and distinct. (See *Writing a Concluding Paragraph*).

- Read several chapters or articles that contain summaries. Go back into the chapters and articles and underline the thesis and topic sentences. Analyze how the writers developed their summaries.

- Keep the summary short and to the point. You are reminding the reader where you have been; you are not repeating every detail.

- Think of a summary as a review of the major points you want to leave with your reader.

TAKING
THE NEXT STEPS

Combining Paragraph Structures

Organizing Multiple Paragraphs

COMBINING PARAGRAPH STRUCTURES

Now that you have practiced the thirty ways to organize and write paragraphs, it is time to take the next step: combining two or more paragraph structures. Good writers are able to combine paragraph structures to suit their particular needs. This process is called "synthesis."

The possible combinations of paragraph structures are endless and perhaps best shown by a few examples. A simple, logical illustration is to combine a descriptive paragraph with a division paragraph. If you recall, in a descriptive paragraph, the writer uses as many of the five senses as possible to describe an object. (See *Writing a Descriptive Paragraph*). In a division paragraph, the writer breaks down a subject into its component parts and then discusses each part. (See *Writing a Paragraph Using Division*). These concepts work effectively together; in a paragraph combining both structures, the writer can describe an object by breaking it down into how it looks, sounds, tastes, smells, and feels, and then discuss each one in turn.

As a second example, you may want to combine the problem and solution paragraph with the climactic paragraph. (See *Writing a Problem and Solution Paragraph* and *Writing a Climactic Paragraph*). Begin by stating the problem. Follow up with solutions that you present from least to most important. Remember to use transitional words and phrases to introduce each solution such as initially, even more important, and most significant of all.

Even though this book focuses on the thirty paragraph structures individually, many of the example paragraphs are actually combination paragraphs. Reread the example paragraphs from a few chapters and identify which paragraph structures are combined.

Writers combine paragraph structures for practical and logical reasons. Practical reasons include the need to present complex ideas in an understandable format and the desire for variety in writing. Combining paragraph structures also takes logical advantage of human nature. Our minds are constantly looking for ways to organize the information we receive. Using several overlapping methods of organization helps readers organize, understand, and remember what they read.

As you learn to combine paragraph structures, you will initially find the practice somewhat difficult. Over time and with experience, the process will become easier. Eventually, it will become second nature, and you will find yourself combining two and three paragraph structures with ease.

ORGANIZING MULTIPLE PARAGRAPHS

Creating a good paragraph is just the first step into the larger world of writing. Once you have mastered the variety of paragraph structures, you can then begin connecting and organizing multiple paragraphs. Learning how to combine multiple paragraphs will help you with longer, more complex pieces of writing such as letters, memos, essays, compositions, reports, or books. Although a thorough discussion of how to write these types of longer pieces is beyond the scope of this book, it is helpful to take a glimpse at this next step in the writing process.

A simple way to organize a composition of between five and seven paragraphs uses the same approach as a paragraph using division. (See *Writing a Paragraph Using Division*). The writer begins with an introductory paragraph, which includes a thesis statement defining the whole composition and additional sentences providing organizational clues. (See *Writing an Introductory Paragraph*). Next, the writer adds the body paragraphs; each body paragraph discusses a subordinate point in the order set forth in the introductory paragraph. Finally, the writer summarizes by reviewing the body paragraphs and then restating the thesis in different words. (See *Writing a Summary Paragraph*). When used in a composition, this method is referred to as "subordination and coordination," because the introductory and summary paragraphs "coordinate" with each other, and the body paragraphs provide the "subordinate" points.

A composition using subordination and coordination looks like this:

INTRODUCTION:
     Thesis statement
     Point 1
     Point 2
     Point 3

BODY PARAGRAPH 1:
     Topic sentence restating Point 1
     Supporting sentences

BODY PARAGRAPH 2:
     Topic sentence restating Point 2
     Supporting sentences

BODY PARAGRAPH 3:
     Topic sentence restating Point 3
     Supporting sentences

SUMMARY PARAGRAPH:
     Point 1
     Point 2
     Point 3
     Restate thesis statement

This composition structure, sometimes called the "five paragraph theme," is a simple yet common approach to writing about more complex ideas. This basic structure—introducing a subject by providing a thesis and organizational clues, discussing the subject in the body, and summarizing the discussion and restating the thesis—applies to writing of almost any length.

A simple way to understand subordination and coordination comes from advice given by veteran speakers: "First, tell the audience what you are going to tell them. Then, tell it to them. Finally, tell them what you just told them." This is an informal way of telling the speaker to provide an introduction, a body, and a summary. The advice applies to writers as well.

Using subordination and coordination is just one of many ways to organize multiple paragraphs into a longer piece of writing. As you begin to move toward more complex written works, remember your most important goal is to help your reader understand the subject. The tools in this book will help, but the real key is practice, practice, practice.

Happy Writing!
Victor C. Pellegrino

INDEX

INDEX

ABOUT THE AUTHOR

Victor C. Pellegrino, Professor Emeritus, taught writing and literature at Maui Community College for twenty-eight years, and served eight years as chairperson of the Language Arts Division. He has also taught upper division classes in advanced writing and American literature for the University of Hawai'i on Maui.

Recognized as a statewide leader in the field of writing, Pellegrino was the first recipient of the Excellence in English Teaching Award presented by the Hawai'i affiliate of the National Council of Teachers of English. He also received the Excellence in Teaching English Award from the Hawai'i Branch of the English-Speaking Union of the United States. Pellegrino has served on the editorial board of Makali'i, The Journal of the University of Hawai'i Community Colleges, and has edited for publication many manuscripts.

During his teaching career, Pellegrino developed a unique interdisciplinary Eastern world literature course emphasizing the writings of India, China, and Japan. This course complemented Pellegrino's Western world literature course emphasizing Europe, Africa, and Russia. He also taught British and American literature.

Pellegrino's books have guided writers for two decades. In 1984, he wrote two books designed for use in Hawai'i schools, *You Can Write! Practical Writing Skills for Hawai'i* and *You Can Write Workbook* (both out-of-print). *A Writer's Guide to Transitional Words and Expressions* was first published in 1987 (8th printing, 2009). *A Writer's Guide to Using Eight Methods of Transition*, published in 1993 (3rd printing, 2008), serves as a complementary text to his popular transitional words book. *A Writer's Guide to Powerful Paragraphs*, his third title in the writer's guide series, was published in 2003 (2nd printing, 2009), and focuses on thirty different ways to organize and write effective paragraphs. In 2006, he added a fourth title to his writing series, *A Writer's Guide to Perfect Punctuation*.

Pellegrino's writings are not limited to the world of English. *Maui Art Thoughts: Expressions and Visions* (out-of-print) focuses on his philosophical aphorisms. *A Slip of Bamboo: A Collection of Haiku from Maui* contains selections from the hundreds of haiku he has been writing since 1973. In 2001, he published an Italian cookbook, *Simply Bruschetta: Garlic Toast the Italian Way*. He completed his first family history, *The Falcone Family (La Famiglia Falcone)* in 2007. He is currently working on a novel, a children's allegory, a vegetable-based Italian cookbook, as well as his second family history, *The Pellegrino Family (La Famiglia Pellegrino)*.

In addition to his own writing, Pellegrino has edited and assisted in the publication of numerous books for authors from Hawai'i and the Mainland as well as conducted self-publishing seminars for Maui Community College's Department of Continuing Education and Hawai'i Writer's Conference. As a cookbook author, Pellegrino has appeared on television shows, in Hawai'i and on the Mainland. He has held numerous food demonstrations, taught many cooking classes, served as guest chef, and conducted cookbook writing workshops.

Pellegrino received B.S. and M.S. degrees from the SUNY, Buffalo. He has studied and traveled extensively in Japan and China. In 1984, he was a Fulbright Scholar in India. He is married to Wallette Garcia. They have three children, Shelley, Angela, and Hōkūao, and two grandchildren, Jonathan and Ryan.

BOOKS BY PELLEGRINO

A Writer's Guide to Transitional Words and Expressions
Pellegrino, © 1987, 1989, 1999; 8th printing, 2009
ISBN 0-945045-02-6, soft cover, $16.95

A Writer's Guide to Using Eight Methods of Transition
Pellegrino, © 1993; 2nd printing, © 2004 (Revised); 3rd printing,
2008, ISBN 0-945045-03-4, soft cover, $12.95

A Writer's Guide to Powerful Paragraphs
Pellegrino, © 2003, 2nd printing, 2009
ISBN 0-945045-05-0, soft cover, $24.95

A Writer's Guide to Perfect Punctuation
Pellegrino, © 2006, ISBN 0-945045-07-7, soft cover, $14.95

A Slip of Bamboo: A Collection of Haiku from Maui
Pellegrino, © 1996, ISBN 0-945045-04-2, soft cover, $9.95

Simply Bruschetta: Garlic Toast the Italian Way
Pellegrino, © 2001, ISBN 0-945045-06-9, hard cover, $18.95

Maui arThoughts: Expressions and Visions
Pellegrino, © 1988, ISBN 0-945045-01-8 (Out of Print)

You Can Write Workbook
Pellegrino, © 1983, ISBN 0-935848-28-2 (Out of Print)

You Can Write! Practical Writing Skills for Hawai'i
Pellegrino, © 1982, ISBN 0-935848-04-5 (Out of Print)

SEE ORDER FORM

Maui arThoughts Company

...the creative publisher with books that work...

P.O. Box 967, Wailuku, HI, USA 96793-0967
Phone/Fax Inquiries: 808-244-0156
Phone/Fax Orders Toll Free: 800-403-3472
E-mail: books@maui.net   Website: www.booksmaui.com

ORDER FORM

● *Order by Mail... Phone... Fax... E-mail... or On-line*

MAIL ORDERS TO: Maui arThoughts Company
　　　　　　　　 P.O. Box 967, Wailuku, HI, USA 96793-0967
PHONE or FAX FOR INFORMATION/INQUIRIES: 808-244-0156
PHONE or FAX ORDERS TOLL FREE: 800-403-3472
E-MAIL ORDERS TO: booksmaui@hawaii.rr.com
WEBSITE: www.booksmaui.com

●PLEASE SEND ME (Indicate Number of Copies in Boxes)

☐	*A Writer's Guide to Powerful Paragraphs* @ $24.95 per copy, ISBN 0-945045-05-0	$ +
☐	*A Writer's Guide to Transitional Words & Expressions* @ $16.95 per copy, ISBN 0-945045-02-6	$ +
☐	*A Writer's Guide to Using Eight Methods of Transition* @ $12.95 per copy, ISBN 0-945045-03-4	$ +
☐	*A Writer's Guide to Perfect Punctuation* @ $14.95 per copy, ISBN 0-945045-07-7	$ +
	SUBTOTAL	$

●DISCOUNTS (Include Purchase Order)

Retail Bookstores, less 40%	$ −
College/University Bookstores, less 20%	$ −
Schools & Libraries, less 10%	$ −

●TAXES

Hawai'i Residents (Include .04166 Sales Tax)	$ +
Hawai'i Bkstrs., Schools & Libraries (Include .005 Whsl. Tax)	$ +

●SHIPPING & HANDLING (2 Choices)

1) For 1 copy: $5.75 USPS Priority Mail. Add $.50 for each　$ +
   additional book up to 10 copies

2) For more than 10 books, we will bill you for S & H.
   Please check your selection below:
   ☐USPS Priority Mail
   ☐UPS 2nd Day Air
   ☐UPS Ground

TOTAL AMOUNT DUE	$

●PAYMENT

Choose to pay now or later. We will bill you for S & H as needed.
☐Check/Money Order (make payable to Maui arThoughts Company)
☐Purchase Order Number (Attach P.O. to Order Form)
☐Bill Me Later

●BILL TO ADDRESS　　　　　●SHIP TO ADDRESS

Name _____　　Name _____

Address_____　　Address_____

City _____ State ___ Zip_____　　City _____ State ___ Zip_____

●NOTE　All prices are subject to change without notice.